WORD
GAMES
FOR
ADULTS

Dr Gareth Moore B.Sc (Hons) M.Phil Ph.D is the internationally best-selling author of a wide range of brain-training and puzzle books for both children and adults, including *Brain Games for Adults, Enigma: Crack the Code, Ultimate Dot to Dot, Brain Games for Clever Kids, Lateral Logic* and *Extreme Mazes*. His books have sold millions of copies in the UK alone, and have been published in over thirty different languages. He is also the creator of online brain-training site BrainedUp.com, and runs the daily puzzle site PuzzleMix.com.

Find him online at DrGarethMoore.com, and on Twitter at @DrGarethMoore.

WORD GAMES FOR ADULTS

DR GARETH MOORE

Michael O'Mara Books Limited

First published in Great Britain in 2022 by
Michael O'Mara Books Limited
9 Lion Yard
Tremadoc Road
London SW4 7NQ

A CIP catalogue record for this book is available from the British
Library.

Papers used by Michael O'Mara Books Limited are natural,
recyclable products made from wood grown in sustainable
forests. The manufacturing processes conform to the
environmental regulations of the country of origin.

ISBN: 978-1-78929-471-2 in paperback print format

2 3 4 5 6 7 8 9 10

Designed and typeset by Gareth Moore
Brain icon in page headers: Visual Generation/Adobe Stock

Printed and bound by CPI Group (UK) Ltd, Croydon, CR0 4YY

www.mombooks.com

INTRODUCTION

Welcome to *Word Games for Adults*, packed from cover to cover with a really wide and varied range of language and vocabulary puzzles.

Some of the more than 30 different puzzle types in this book will be familiar, while others are likely to be new to you. No matter the type, however, it's worth giving everything a go – your brain thrives on novelty, after all!

The puzzles are arranged in no particular order, so feel free to dip in as you please. Some of the types are easier than others, with the simplest probably being the anagram pages, while the trickiest are surely the cryptic crosswords.

If you ever get stuck on a puzzle then feel free to take a quick peek at the solutions – or have someone else do it for you – and add in some extra clues to get you going. You can of course also use the solutions to check your answers. Most of the puzzles have a unique solution, although occasionally you may find other words that fit the clues – particularly for the word ladder puzzles in which you must convert one word into another. This occasional alternative route is hard to avoid, given the over 280,000 words in the Oxford English Dictionary!

Most of all, remember that the puzzles are meant to be fun – so, if you ever find yourself getting too frustrated, simply skip the puzzle in question or try it again another day.

Dr Gareth Moore

Find the listed words **all related to the universe** written in the grid in any direction, including diagonally.

R	S	R	A	T	S	V	M	C	P	T	L	C	C	A
E	P	U	I	R	N	B	E	H	D	G	E	Q	S	S
I	T	E	C	A	P	S	O	A	A	R	U	A	B	M
N	H	T	H	A	R	T	R	L	K	A	I	L	I	O
E	G	A	I	N	O	K	A	A	S	E	A	L	A	T
B	I	M	E	N	M	X	R	A	A	C	K	I	M	A
U	L	U	S	A	I	G	R	V	K	Y	I	U	P	I
L	W	T	T	E	N	S	O	H	W	N	I	E	H	L
A	A	T	S	A	S	N	O	A	S	L	M	L	E	P
E	E	M	B	D	R	L	Y	A	E	S	G	S	H	L
R	S	G	I	E	E	O	E	H	L	O	L	I	W	A
E	I	O	P	S	R	E	T	S	U	L	C	M	N	N
B	V	U	T	I	M	E	V	E	R	B	S	A	P	E
N	S	Y	A	N	T	I	M	A	T	T	E	R	B	T
X	I	T	A	H	Y	D	R	O	G	E	N	O	L	S

ANTIMATTER
ATOMS
BIG BANG
BLACK HOLES
CLUSTERS
DARK MATTER
GALAXIES
HELIUM
HYDROGEN
LIGHT

MILKY WAY
NEBULAE
PHOTONS
PLANETS
QUASARS
SPACE
STARS
SUPERNOVAE
TIME
VOIDS

Time: _____

Place all of the listed words into the grid, crossword-style.

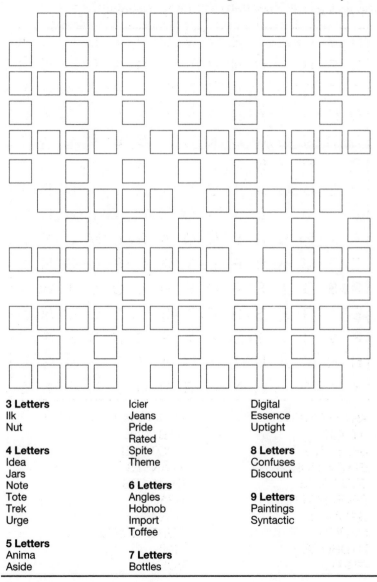

3 Letters
Ilk
Nut

4 Letters
Idea
Jars
Note
Tote
Trek
Urge

5 Letters
Anima
Aside

Icier
Jeans
Pride
Rated
Spite
Theme

6 Letters
Angles
Hobnob
Import
Toffee

7 Letters
Bottles

Digital
Essence
Uptight

8 Letters
Confuses
Discount

9 Letters
Paintings
Syntactic

Solve the clues to write a word on each row, one letter per block. Each row contains the same letters as the previous row, plus one extra letter – but the letters may be in a different order.

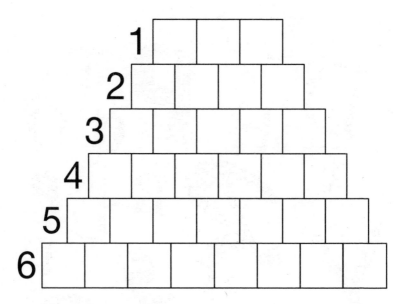

1. Gone off

2. Small amounts

3. Situated

4. Dwellings

5. Bragged

6. Most wide-ranging

Can you rearrange these letters to reveal four **flowers**? Each letter will be used exactly once, with no letters left over.

How many words can you form that use the middle letter plus two or more of the other letters? No letter may be used more times than it appears within the circle. There is one word that uses all nine letters.

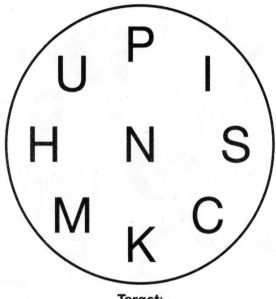

Target:
35 words

For each line, find a word of the indicated length that can both join to the end of the preceding word to make a new word, and join to the start of the following word to make a new word. For example, OUT _ _ _ _ LED could be joined with GROW to make OUTGROW and GROWLED.

PROOF   _ _ _ _   JUST

NOW   _ _ _ _   AFTER

POST   _ _ _ _ _ _   PIECE

CON   _ _ _   TAIL

CROSS   _ _ _   LED

Find the listed words **as cross shapes**, either as a + or ×. Half the word forms one arm of the cross; the other half of the word forms the other. One letter is shared by both halves.

A	D	S	E	T	P	U	U	A	A	S	Q	E	D	M
I	L	S	Z	O	U	T	A	Y	T	D	V	N	B	A
P	R	E	P	O	T	A	A	D	E	Q	U	B	L	Q
S	P	S	U	S	T	M	D	E	L	L	E	O	O	I
E	U	S	R	A	M	A	L	G	Y	B	L	A	C	K
E	M	O	I	S	T	T	E	T	R	H	V	R	E	O
E	L	B	Z	O	R	E	S	T	R	G	Y	D	P	E
O	Y	A	E	E	T	A	N	U	A	T	A	V	R	P
H	U	L	L	A	S	N	P	I	E	H	U	E	A	S
W	E	O	M	P	E	T	U	L	C	P	E	R	S	E
L	L	O	I	A	U	L	T	E	I	A	N	E	E	E
S	Y	Y	L	T	O	Y	M	T	V	E	L	D	E	D
L	D	A	L	I	E	N	D	E	A	C	T	E	S	D
E	M	E	V	O	A	O	A	T	T	L	R	Y	E	D
A	U	I	D	N	T	S	E	D	E	U	P	R	T	M

ADEQUATELY	MOISTURIZE
ALIENATION	OUTPUT
AMALGAMATE	PERSEVERED
BLACKBOARD	PETULANTLY
DEACTIVATE	PREPOSSESS
ENRAPTURED	PURSUE
HULLABALOO	REDEEM
MECHANICAL	SLOWLY

Solve the clues to complete this crossword.

Across
1 Arrogant (4)
4 Hallucination (8)
8 Not out (2,4)
9 Fastened with a metal spike (6)
10 Shortly (4)
11 Sever (5,3)
13 Relatively (13)
16 Visual balance (8)
19 Smell strongly and unpleasantly (4)
20 Supplication (6)
22 Cure-all (6)
23 Intensely preoccupied (8)
24 Clothes (4)

Down
2 A set of foundation stories (9)
3 Adult (5-2)
4 Nerd (5)
5 Lax (7)
6 Stench (5)
7 Lyric poem (3)
12 Percolating (9)
14 Comes back (7)
15 Decision (7)
17 Perhaps (5)
18 Give up (5)
21 One of a series of bones attached to the spine (3)

Find a hidden five-letter word, based on the mildly cryptic clue. Four incorrect guesses have already been made, and the individual letters in each guess marked as either:

- Correct, and in the right position, marked in black
- Correct, but in the wrong position, marked in grey
- Not in the word, marked with a white background

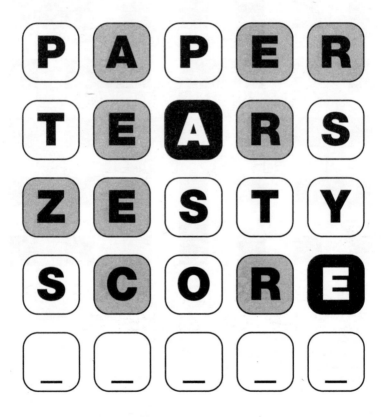

Clue: It's enjoyed with a passion

Delete one letter from each of the pairs below to reveal five hidden words.

CP EL UO RN DE

GN NI NO MJ AO

DP LR AO LG OE LN

DP IL NA TO SI AN EU ML

FC UO NU DN TA ME ER
NP OT AI NE TL

Solve this crossword which has all of its clues written within the grid.

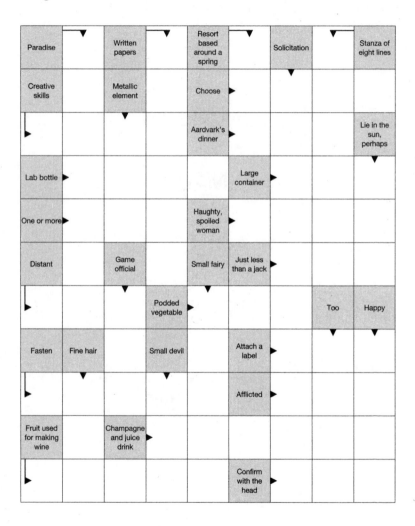

Paradise	▼	Written papers	▼	Resort based around a spring	▼	Solicitation	▼	Stanza of eight lines
Creative skills		Metallic element		Choose ▶	▼			
▶		▼		Aardvark's dinner ▶				Lie in the sun, perhaps
Lab bottle ▶					Large container ▶			▼
One or more ▶				Haughty, spoiled woman ▶				
Distant		Game official		Small fairy	Just less than a jack ▶			
▶		▼	Podded vegetable ▶	▼			Too	Happy
Fasten	Fine hair		Small devil		Attach a label ▶		▼	▼
▶	▼		▼		Afflicted ▶			
Fruit used for making wine		Champagne and juice drink ▶						
▶					Confirm with the head ▶			

Each of the following words is missing its first and last letter, which must – for each word – be identical. For example, _XAMPL_ could be solved with 'E', to give 'EXAMPLE'.

NORE

RMAD

HEF

_HI_

_AU_

Can you find a **bird** hidden within all of the following phrases? Each bird must have at least four letters, and will be formed of continuous letters. For example, 'Please deco**de mo**st of them' contains 'demo', as highlighted.

1. He watched warily as the wasp, arrow-like barb at the ready, headed straight for him.

2. She stared curiously at the celebrity heartthrob in the store – what were they doing here?

3. The typical farmyard pig, eons ago, had once been a wild boar

4. They were photographed crossing the road, with the star lingering until the flashbulbs had all gone off.

5. A new Renaissance began on the very day they first unveiled her great artwork.

Find the listed **shades of red** written in the grid in any direction, including diagonally. Some of the words 'wrap around' the edges of the puzzle, continuing as if the puzzle repeated edge-to-edge forever.

```
R  R  A  A  I  E  S  A  N  V
E  L  D  M  N  B  I  C  D  R
F  R  S  I  N  P  R  D  Y  M
A  O  M  R  N  S  E  N  S  I
N  R  U  I  G  A  C  A  Y  C
A  B  O  A  L  R  L  I  B  A
U  R  R  O  B  I  R  L  U  C
L  N  L  C  N  Y  O  E  R  A
E  A  H  E  E  R  C  N  G  C
A  E  V  M  T  R  E  R  U  T
```

AUBURN	FLAME
BURGUNDY	GARNET
CARDINAL	LAVA
CARMINE	MAROON
CARNELIAN	RASPBERRY
CERISE	RUBY
CHERRY	SCARLET
CRIMSON	VERMILION

Time: _____

In this coded crossword, every letter has been replaced by a number. Each number represents a different letter of the alphabet. Crack the code to complete the crossword.

	15		19		1		13		10		23	
11	17	25 O	6	19	13		16	8	25	7	16	20
	5		25		2		14		5		22	
12	6	16	4		21	19	6	16	9	25	5	2
	17				3		16		12		19	
1	5	25	13	1	16	21	6	12	8	16		
	16		21						16		19	
		26	12	18	18 L	12	15	9	15	16	13	13
	21		16		25		19				3	
20	25	26	15	1	25	17	5		24	17 U	6	13
	2		21		7		5		16		5	
10	18	16	16	21	16		25	1	16	5	19	13
	2		13		20		26		5		2	

1	2	3	4	5	6	7	8	9	10	11	12	13
14	15	16	17	18	19	20	21	22	23	24	25	26

A B C D E F G H I J K L M N O P Q R S T U V W X Y Z

Write a letter in each shaded square, to form seven words. The last two letters of each word form the first two letters of the following word, in the same order, as indicated by the shaded lines.

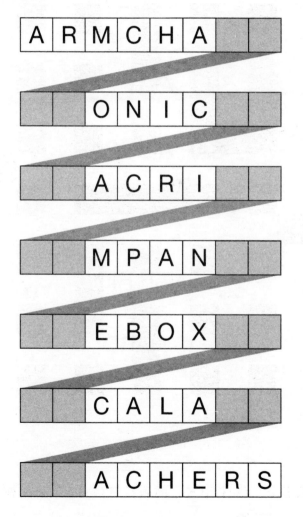

| A | R | M | C | H | A | | |

| | | O | N | I | C | | |

| | | A | C | R | I | | |

| | | M | P | A | N | | |

| | | E | B | O | X | | |

| | | C | A | L | A | | |

| | | A | C | H | E | R | S |

Unscramble the following anagrammed words to reveal five
root vegetables. Ignore any spaces.

AMY

SAP A SUGAR

I NOON

SNAP RIP

IS HARD

Find as many words as you can by starting on any letter and tracing a path to touching squares, including diagonally touching squares. Do not revisit any square within a word. There is one word that uses all of the letters.

O	Z	D
R	I	E
T	A	P

Target:
45 words

Half of the letters have been deleted from each of the following words. Can you restore them in order to reveal five **ball games**?

_R_Q_E_

_E_N_S

H_C_E_

_U_B_

_A_E_A_L

See how quickly you can complete this smaller, break-time crossword.

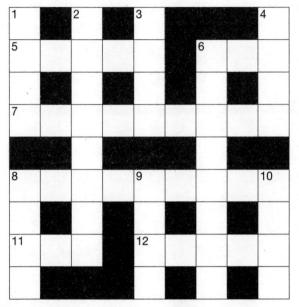

Across
5 Bodily thrust (5)
6 Hand over money for something (3)
7 Surgical procedure (9)
8 Study of the universe (9)
11 Used to exist (3)
12 Bank official (5)

Down
1 Voice between soprano and tenor (4)
2 Perfumed smokes (8)
3 Million, as a prefix (4)
4 Religious song (4)
6 Captive (8)
8 Hooded monk's habit (4)
9 Social, black-and-white whale (4)
10 Tibetan oxen (4)

Find the listed **biology-related** words written in the grid in any direction, including diagonally.

```
E G N S L E S I S O T I M U R
E O L T L I E O R G A N I S M
E C I E N S Y M B I O S I S O
M O E M E E M O L E C U L E G
S R G C S L U E S N L E O E Y
C M I E O I O R T I B I I Y B
I O O L N S S U O O S U P N A
G H M L E E Y O C N G O Y I I
L E M Y Z N E S I A B Y M Y D
O I G E N O M E T E V G Z S E
P H E R O M O N E E M E N V O
E M O I B O N R E O M Y E A E
S E E O O T A T I B A H N O B
O N O I T U L O V E A O H A S
I O E M E N O M R O H C I A L
```

BIOME
ECOSYSTEM
ENZYME
EVOLUTION
GENE
GENOME
HABITAT
HORMONE
LIPID
MEIOSIS

MITOSIS
MOLECULE
NEURON
ORGANISM
OSMOSIS
PHEROMONE
STEM CELL
SYMBIOSIS
VACUOLE
ZYGOTE

Time: _____

Place all of the listed words into the grid, crossword-style.

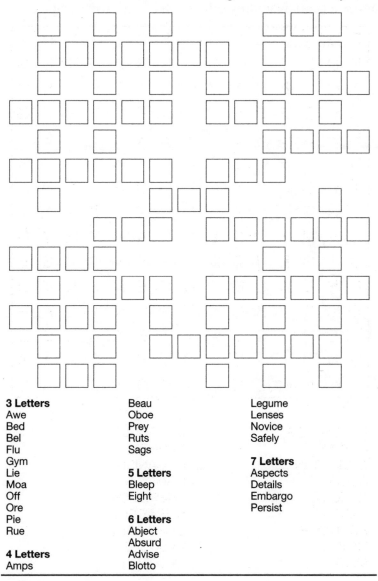

3 Letters
Awe
Bed
Bel
Flu
Gym
Lie
Moa
Off
Ore
Pie
Rue

4 Letters
Amps

Beau
Oboe
Prey
Ruts
Sags

5 Letters
Bleep
Eight

6 Letters
Abject
Absurd
Advise
Blotto

Legume
Lenses
Novice
Safely

7 Letters
Aspects
Details
Embargo
Persist

Solve the clues to write a word on each row, one letter per block. Each row contains the same letters as the previous row, plus one extra letter – but the letters may be in a different order.

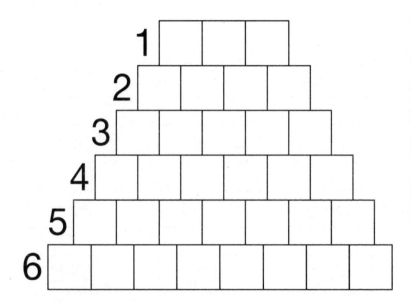

1. Brewed drink

2. Rip

3. Super

4. Shredded, as food

5. Allowed

6. Incline

Rearrange these boxes to spell out five **items of stationery**. Each box will be used exactly once.

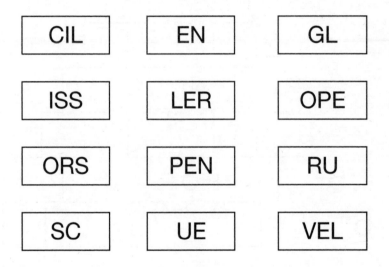

CIL   EN   GL

ISS   LER   OPE

ORS   PEN   RU

SC   UE   VEL

Can you identify all five of the following **movies**, for which only the initial letters of their titles are given? The length of each word is also indicated.

B A T F T M
(4, 3, 3, 4, 3, 5)

A F
(7, 4)

B O P
(5, 2, 4)

N T T D
(2, 4, 2, 3)

S T H
(5, 3, 8)

For each line, find a word of the indicated length that can both join to the end of the preceding word to make a new word, and join to the start of the following word to make a new word. For example, OUT _ _ _ _ LED could be joined with GROW to make OUTGROW and GROWLED.

COIN   _ _ _   LONG

MAY   _ _ _   LOCK

SUB   _ _ _ _   LIGHT

FORE   _ _ _ _ _   AGE

OUT   _ _ _ _   SLASH

Find all these words **containing 'ACE'** in the grid in any direction. The middle of the grid has been hidden, however, and it is up to you to identify these 25 missing letters.

```
R  E  C  A  R  B  N  I  A  M  C  A  A  L  E
R  E  C  A  R  B  M  E  P  A  C  E  D  T  O
H  E  S  R  O  H  E  C  A  R  F  C  A  R  L
T  R  E  S  U  R  F  A  C  E  B  B  C  E  T
E  C  A  L  P  E  R  I  F  A  R  O  U  A  E
B  I  R  T  H                 M  N  D  C  P
E  P  R  E  F                 T  J  A  R  B
C  D  F  A  C                 A  F  T  F  A
A  E  N  T  C                 R  C  Y  R  C
N  X  P  A  L                 F  E  P  C  K
R  K  E  K  C  L  E  N  T  L  E  C  E  A  S
U  P  C  T  A  A  C  N  L  B  R  A  F  L  P
F  E  A  C  B  Y  I  A  A  A  A  L  A  R  A
N  F  E  L  C  O  N  B  E  N  C  A  C  B  C
R  A  E  R  O  S  P  A  C  E  N  P  E  A  E
```

ADJACENCY	MAINBRACE
AEROSPACE	NECKLACE
BACKSPACE	PACED
BIRTHPLACE	PALACE
COMMONPLACE	PEACE
EMBRACE	PREFACE
EXACERBATE	RACEHORSE
FIREPLACE	RESURFACE
FURNACE	TYPEFACE
INTERFACE	UNTRACEABLE

Solve the clues to complete this crossword.

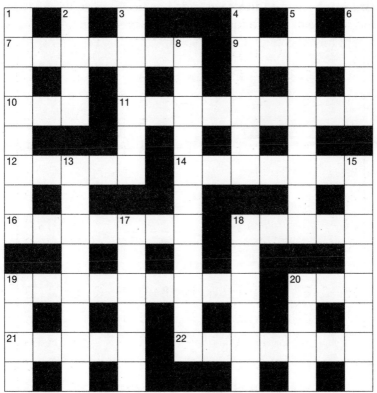

Across

7 Least amount possible (7)
9 Existing (5)
10 Set up (3)
11 Governed by bishops (9)
12 Dirty looks (5)
14 Seven-piece shape puzzle (7)
16 Pain-relief tablet (7)
18 Sugary (5)
19 Haughtiness (9)
20 Material thrown from a volcano (3)
21 Large country house (5)
22 Command level (7)

Down

1 Keeps you dry (8)
2 Tight; close-fitting (4)
3 Glowing fire remnants (6)
4 Small bird of prey (6)
5 Scatter (8)
6 Worn to conceal the face (4)
8 Upkeep (11)
13 Running out (8)
15 Equal in design (8)
17 Esteem (6)
18 Fume (6)
19 Food given to poor people (4)
20 Compatriot (4)

Crack the letter-shift code in order to identify five **things you might find at a fairground**. The same code is used for all five lines. For example, 'A' might have become 'B'; 'B' might have become 'C'; and so on.

BANNEO SDAAH

YWNKQOAH

YHKSJ

DWQJPAZ DKQOA

NKHHAN YKWOPAN

A	B	C	D	E	F	G	H	I	J	K	L	M

N	O	P	Q	R	S	T	U	V	W	X	Y	Z

Unscramble the following anagrammed '+1' words to reveal five **famous rivers**. Each line has had **one extra letter added**, however, which is not part of the anagram. Read all these extracted letters in order from top-to-bottom to reveal a sixth river. Ignore any spaces in the anagrams.

I AM AN OZ

LINEN

DOOR ICON

A BUN DUE

SIR HEN

Can you solve this cryptic crossword?
For clue format help, see **en.wikipedia.org/wiki/Cryptic_crossword**

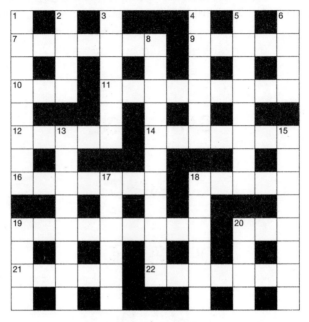

Across

7 Revolutionary company hoarding exotic grain characterizing a type of food? (7)
9 A thing requiring opening to get semi-precious stone (5)
10 Soft fruit is fine in general as starters (3)
11 Mindset encountered around northern Italy possibly (9)
12 Tab kept by tombola belittled (5)
14 One suspect trainee mostly showing apathy (7)
16 Busy creature receiving special approval to be individually tailored? (7)
18 Rex in a drinking bout has to give way suddenly (5)
19 A game broadcast in a bit – what's that? (4,5)
20 Skirt left out as equipment (3)
21 Time taken by Goan when moving in dance (5)
22 Intellectual, say, associated with good leader (7)

Down

1 Driver, perhaps, to leave liberal fellow on strike (4,4)
2 Try to impress a beginner in golf that's eagerly expectant (4)
3 Term among the Spanish for a protective covering (6)
4 Show in public a group of shops? (6)
5 Artist, Dutch, with unconventional trio keeping a source of heat (8)
6 Casual drink in a group (4)
8 Desecration to be repaired? That's thoughtful (11)
13 Same rogue beset by tendency in underground area? (8)
15 A fool amid playing of duet shows point of view (8)
17 One giving a speech for a Tory essentially (6)
18 Begin somehow to enclose note? That's kind (6)
19 Pleasing accent after leaving area (4)
20 Joint in park needed (4)

Can you identify all of the following **national airlines**, each of which has had all of its vowels deleted? Can you also say which country they are the flag carrier for?

STRN RLNS

R PCFC

CLNDR

LTL

BR

WORD GAME 33

Time: _____

Find the listed **shades of purple** written in the grid in any direction, including diagonally. Some of the words 'wrap around' the edges of the puzzle, continuing as if the puzzle repeated edge-to-edge forever.

```
E  N  D  E  R  Y  O  L  A  V
D  A  N  G  O  I  Y  F  A  N
O  V  M  F  S  P  N  R  O  E
M  O  I  E  U  I  A  D  R  R
C  A  R  O  T  C  R  N  I  E
B  H  U  A  L  H  H  I  S  G
O  L  I  V  M  E  Y  S  N  Y
T  I  U  D  E  L  T  S  I  H
P  L  U  M  A  G  E  N  T  A
W  I  S  T  E  R  I  A  V  I
```

AMETHYST	MAUVE
FANDANGO	MULBERRY
FUCHSIA	ORCHID
INDIGO	PANSY
IRIS	PLUM
LAVENDER	THISTLE
MAGENTA	VIOLET
MAROON	WISTERIA

WORD GAME 34

Time: _____

In this coded crossword, every letter has been replaced by a number. Each number represents a different letter of the alphabet. Crack the code to complete the crossword.

	6	9	19	24	14	11	8		26	18	23	18
18		18		2		14			6		24	
4	8	15	9	8		20	8	15	16	14 (I)	15	12
4		10 (T)		11		20		8			10	
6	5	11	13		4	18	11	8	1	8	6	16
25		14		25		15		16		21		
	6	7	14	6	15		20	25	14	10	3	
		8		24		20		8		11		16
18	11	16	14	15	6	11	13		26	8	10	8
	8			9		14		6		26		25
22	6	10	9	1	8	16		2 (S)	1	14	11	10
	9		6			12		17		2		6
5	1	14	26		5	8	20	2	14	10	8	

1	2	3	4	5	6	7	8	9	10	11	12	13
14	15	16	17	18	19	20	21	22	23	24	25	26

A B C D E F G H I J K L M N O P Q R S T U V W X Y Z

Write a letter in each shaded square, to form seven words. The last two letters of each word form the first two letters of the following word, in the same order, as indicated by the shaded lines.

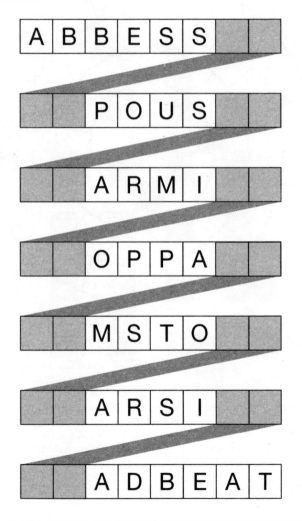

A	B	B	E	S	S		
		P	O	U	S		
		A	R	M	I		
		O	P	P	A		
		M	S	T	O		
		A	R	S	I		
		A	D	B	E	A	T

Each letter in this spiral crossword is clued twice: once reading inwards, and once reading outwards.

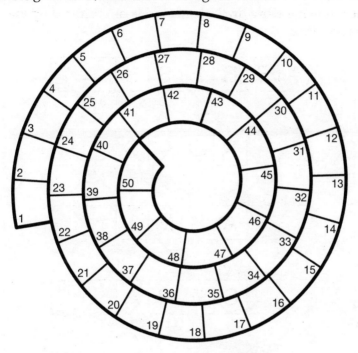

	Inward		**Outward**
1-5	Sets of cards	**50-47**	Assistant
6-12	Takes aggressive military action	**46-39**	Substance
		38-34	Paparazzi target
13-18	Emerged	**33-27**	A branch of mathematics
19-23	Automaton	**26-22**	Verve
24-28	Natural sweetener	**21-17**	Endured
29-31	Entreat	**16-14**	Knight's title
32-36	Tag	**13-11**	Put a question to
37-42	Cream-filled cake	**10-8**	Feline animal
43-45	Letter after zeta	**7-4**	Chore
46-50	Newspapers and television in general	**3-1**	Soft, flat hat

Can you find the word **'HIDING'** in this network? Start on any circle and then follow lines to touching circles, spelling out the word circle by circle. No circle can be revisited.

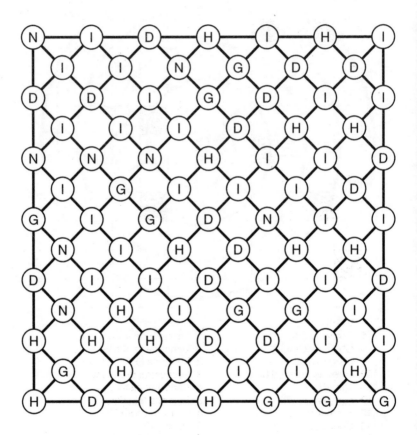

Time: _____

To complete this crossword you must not only solve the clues but also add the missing shaded squares and clue numbers to the grid. The shading has rotational symmetry.

Across
1 Courtesy (10)
6 Change title (6)
7 Land measure (4)
10 Large-leaved, edible plant (7)
12 Forty winks (3)
13 Excavate (3)
14 Conflagration (7)
15 Comfort (4)
18 Mexican national flower (6)
19 Cave dweller (10)

Down
1 Bird in a pear tree, in a Christmas song (9)
2 Tongues (9)
3 Orchestral drum set (7)
4 Period of history (3)
5 Knight's title (3)
8 From the core (9)
9 Spying (9)
11 Large wild ox (7)
16 Subjective subject (3)
17 Id counterpart (3)

Link the top word to the bottom word by writing a word
on each step, changing just one letter at a time while also
possibly rearranging the letters. For example, you could
change CAT to COT, then to DOT and finally to DOG.

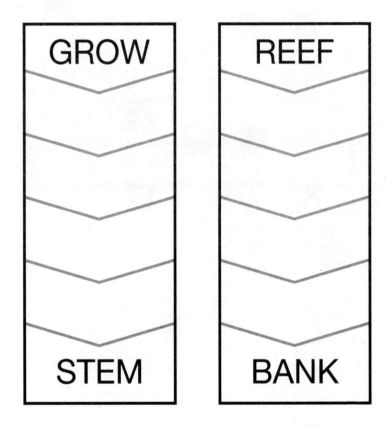

GROW

STEM

REEF

BANK

Time: _____

How many different five-letter words can you spell using this word slider? Imagine sliding each of the tabs up and down to reveal different letters through the central window. One word is spelled already.

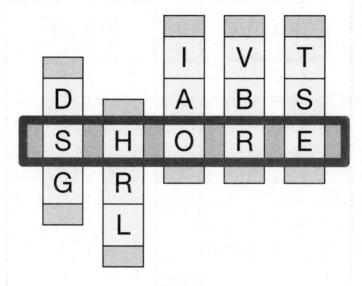

Target:
20 words

Find the listed **symmetrical things** written in the grid in any direction, including diagonally.

S	U	L	A	T	E	C	I	R	C	L	E	W	E	W
P	L	J	L	S	O	L	I	R	E	H	S	A	W	H
H	F	E	I	E	O	R	E	T	T	E	L	E	T	C
E	O	S	L	R	C	E	D	T	L	A	S	T	R	R
R	O	E	L	G	E	B	W	N	T	S	O	I	A	A
E	T	C	B	A	N	W	M	A	O	E	M	K	E	O
B	B	M	R	H	H	A	O	O	A	M	R	E	H	S
U	A	E	B	R	B	A	T	T	C	A	A	W	T	L
T	L	G	S	A	L	O	M	C	L	Y	O	I	R	S
T	L	L	Q	B	T	E	A	J	E	E	E	D	D	O
E	F	A	U	Y	A	O	S	I	A	R	F	N	E	E
R	I	S	A	R	R	R	I	A	R	T	R	F	O	R
F	E	S	R	S	K	K	A	K	V	E	E	A	I	H
L	L	E	E	B	E	K	A	L	F	W	O	N	S	E
Y	D	S	R	A	L	U	C	O	N	I	B	U	A	G

ARCH
BINOCULARS
BUTTERFLY
CIRCLE
DIAMOND
EIFFEL TOWER
FOOTBALL FIELD
GLASSES
HEART
HONEYCOMB CELL

KITE
LETTER O
LETTER W
RECTANGLE
SNOWFLAKE
SPHERE
SQUARE
TAJ MAHAL
VASE
WASHER

Time: _____

Place all of the listed words into the grid, crossword-style.

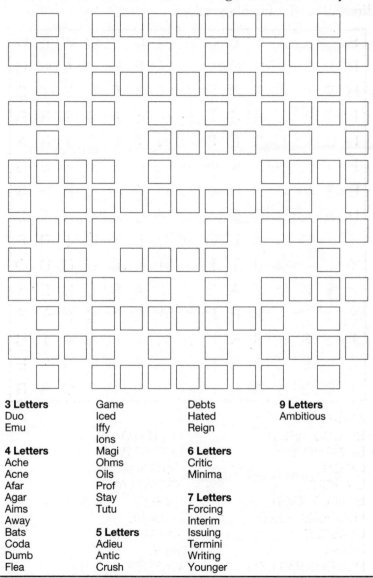

3 Letters
Duo
Emu

4 Letters
Ache
Acne
Afar
Agar
Aims
Away
Bats
Coda
Dumb
Flea

Game
Iced
Iffy
Ions
Magi
Ohms
Oils
Prof
Stay
Tutu

5 Letters
Adieu
Antic
Crush

Debts
Hated
Reign

6 Letters
Critic
Minima

7 Letters
Forcing
Interim
Issuing
Termini
Writing
Younger

9 Letters
Ambitious

Solve the clues to write a word on each row, one letter per block. Each row contains the same letters as the previous row, plus one extra letter – but the letters may be in a different order.

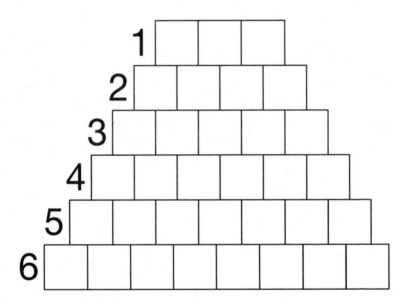

1. Consumed

2. Direction

3. Speed

4. Immerses in water

5. Inhalations

6. Most brazen

Can you rearrange these letters to reveal four **musical instruments**? Each letter will be used exactly once, with no letters left over.

Time: _____

How many words can you form that use the middle letter plus two or more of the other letters? No letter may be used more times than it appears within the circle. There is one word that uses all nine letters.

Target:
40 words

For each line, find a word of the indicated length that can both join to the end of the preceding word to make a new word, and join to the start of the following word to make a new word. For example, OUT _ _ _ _ LED could be joined with GROW to make OUTGROW and GROWLED.

JAIL   _ _ _ _   TABLE

WAR   _ _ _ _   WAY

MAS   _ _ _   TON

MIST   _ _ _ _   PROOF

FOOTS   _ _ _ _   BAR

Find the listed words **written in tight spirals**, as per the example. All the spirals read outwards from the middle.

S	C	E	I	N	G	K	E	I	T	V	O	L	I	G
A	T	I	N	T	W	L	R	N	E	E	R	U	C	E
I	L	E	R	U	N	C	T	N	N	O	I	T	O	N
U	G	E	N	E	E	I	G	N	C	I	N	C	C	A
G	N	A	T	L	C	R	N	U	U	W	D	T	I	O
T	I	N	C	E	L	T	I	L	R	E	S	A	R	N
S	T	G	U	O	P	V	N	L	I	N	G	T	O	O
I	W	Y	R	A	T	I	E	L	S	W	C	I	C	A
T	W	Y	Y	G	I	G	N	E	V	I	W	N	N	O
I	V	I	R	N	O	E	L	I	L	T	T	E	E	E
T	G	C	C	O	N	C	C	H	L	E	P	I	Y	I
C	N	I	L	I	O	N	O	C	E	U	O	R	S	N
N	T	W	I	T	C	V	A	R	A	S	C	R	T	L
L	N	E	N	U	L	O	A	T	O	K	C	E	W	G
V	E	T	E	R	C	O	L	O	L	R	O	W	C	E

CIRCLING	PIROUETTE
COCHLEAR	REVOLUTION
CONVOLUTION	ROTATION
CORKSCREW	SWIVELLING
ENCIRCLE	TURNING
ENTANGLE	TWISTING
ENTWINE	UNCURLING
GYRATION	WINDS

Time: _____

Solve the clues to complete this crossword.

Across
1 Balancing amounts (7)
5 Amplify (5)
9 Amusement (13)
10 Wishing (8)
11 Decomposes (4)
12 Cease business (5,4)
16 Platform for loading ships (4)
17 Contours (8)
19 Elucidation (13)
21 Higher (5)
22 Extremely stupid (7)

Down
2 Digit (6)
3 For a particular purpose (9)
4 All together, in music (5)
6 Omega, to a scientist (3)
7 Mental health (6)
8 Surrounded (6)
11 Edited (9)
13 Shows scorn (6)
14 Sated (4,2)
15 Lament (6)
18 Small nails (5)
20 Grass related to barley and wheat (3)

Find a hidden five-letter word, based on the mildly cryptic clue. Four incorrect guesses have already been made, and the individual letters in each guess marked as either:

- Correct, and in the right position, marked in black
- Correct, but in the wrong position, marked in grey
- Not in the word, marked with a white background

S T A R E

B L A M E

P R I N T

G L I D E

_ _ _ _ _

Clue: It's true, so it's said

Delete one letter from each of the pairs below to reveal five hidden words.

GJ EL OW EA LV

TL RE OI PN IA RD ED

SC LP ER AV EN DR

PC IR IT NA TC AI OT NE

DR YE VN AE AM IL KE DS

Solve this crossword which has all of its clues written within the grid.

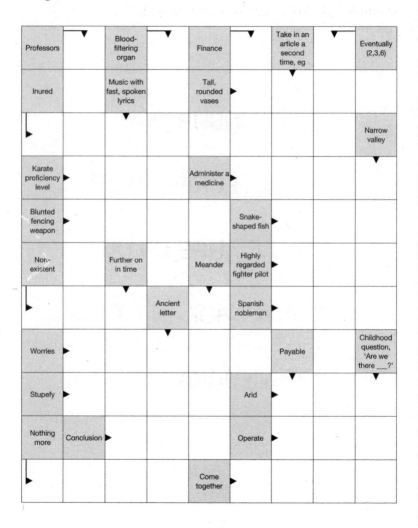

Each of the following words is missing its first and last letter, which must – for each word – be identical. For example, _XAMPL_ could be solved with 'E', to give 'EXAMPLE'.

NSUR

ECKE

AURE

HOE

URRA

Can you find an **elemental metal** hidden within all of the following phrases? Each metal must have at least four letters, and will be formed of continuous letters. For example, 'Please deco**de mo**st of them' contains 'demo', as highlighted.

1. Unfortunately, every sample of topaz included the same flaws

2. Until the demise of the Mongol dynasty, it was the largest continuous land empire in history

3. It's certainly been my culinary experience that each utensil very much has its own role

4. In my complex music setup, the soundbar I umbilically linked to the amplifier was critical

5. At the end of each day, I love to sit on my swinging chair on the patio

Find the listed **shades of yellow** written in the grid in any direction, including diagonally. Some of the words 'wrap around' the edges of the puzzle, continuing as if the puzzle repeated edge-to-edge forever.

P	F	D	E	O	T	U	O	D	N
A	U	R	S	A	L	R	B	L	E
A	D	C	O	L	I	D	O	F	F
N	E	M	R	N	E	R	G	N	C
S	U	U	M	E	O	M	E	D	H
T	Q	S	I	O	T	A	O	B	A
R	S	T	R	B	B	T	O	N	M
A	I	A	P	R	L	A	U	S	P
W	B	R	C	F	E	O	N	B	A
F	S	D	G	I	F	W	N	A	G

AMBER	DAFFODIL
BANANA	GOLD
BISQUE	LEMON
BLONDE	MUSTARD
BUFF	PRIMROSE
BUTTERCUP	SAFFRON
CHAMPAGNE	STRAW
CITRON	SUNFLOWER

Time: _____

In this coded crossword, every letter has been replaced by a number. Each number represents a different letter of the alphabet. Crack the code to complete the crossword.

	24		13	12	8	15	12	24	20		26 **M**
23	6	20	6		15		26		6	11	9	16
	3		24	5	6	14	1	5	2		23	
10	6	26	14		16		12		9	1	9	24
	13			20	9	23	25		12		21
13	9	3	12		15				12	13	17	5
6		12	20	25	26	5	10	5	17	25		18
9	5	20	6				12		17	10	12	12
24		4		24	10	6	20				22	
12	4	21	5		6		20		12	19	12	13
	7		15	16 **N**	23	13	12	24 **S**	24		4	
20	6	10	4		12		13		14	12	20	24
	13		21	5	16	12	24	20	25		24	

1	2	3	4	5	6	7	8	9	10	11	12	13
14	15	16	17	18	19	20	21	22	23	24	25	26

A B C D E F G H I J K L M N O P Q R S T U V W X Y Z

Write a letter in each shaded square, to form seven words.
The last two letters of each word form the first two letters of
the following word, in the same order, as indicated by the
shaded lines.

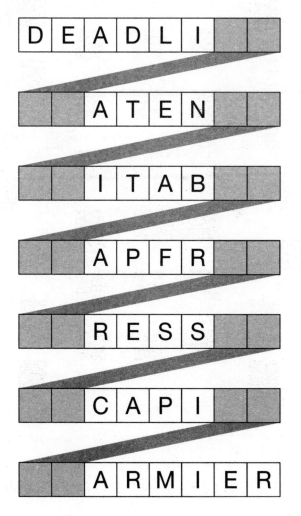

| D | E | A | D | L | I | | |

| | | A | T | E | N | |

| | | I | T | A | B | | |

| | | A | P | F | R | |

| | | R | E | S | S | |

| | | C | A | P | I | |

| | | A | R | M | I | E | R |

Unscramble the following anagrammed words to reveal five **bread products**. Ignore any spaces.

GABLE

NANA

STAR COINS

RICE HOB

BAIT A CAT

Find as many words as you can by starting on any letter and tracing a path to touching squares, including diagonally touching squares. Do not revisit any square within a word. There is one word that uses all of the letters.

Target:
25 words

Half of the letters have been deleted from each of the
following words. Can you restore them in order to reveal
five **musical terms**?

I_P_O_I_A_I_N

_R_A_G_M_N_

_C_I_E_T_L

D_S_O_A_C_

_N_E_V_L

See how quickly you can complete this smaller, break-time crossword.

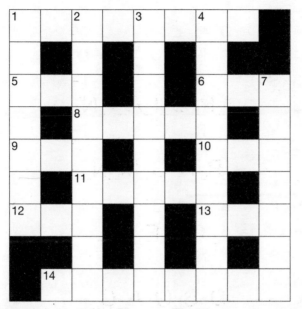

Across

1 Concluding (8)
5 Supernatural creature (3)
6 Rested in a chair (3)
8 Group of ships (5)
9 Prosecute (3)
10 'That's it!' (3)
11 Type of medical dialysis (5)
12 Greek letter before chi (3)
13 Talk endlessly (3)
14 Unlettered (8)

Down

1 Wear your best clothes (5,2)
2 At odds with something (9)
3 Arrive and depart as you please (4,3,2)
4 Wistful thoughts (9)
7 Public transport (7)

Find the listed **peaceful scenes or things** written in the grid in any direction, including diagonally.

K	S	D	E	L	D	N	A	C	E	A	E	E	F	S
S	A	L	A	D	M	E	A	D	O	W	P	A	L	N
A	A	S	T	R	E	A	M	L	U	O	L	A	W	I
L	S	S	E	V	A	W	O	A	C	L	M	A	O	S
E	S	I	Q	A	R	G	S	S	I	I	O	Q	B	U
D	L	M	M	V	F	U	O	N	N	Z	I	U	N	N
N	F	O	S	I	N	D	G	A	W	E	S	A	I	S
A	L	L	R	R	I	L	G	A	L	N	L	R	A	E
L	A	E	I	E	E	N	T	S	O	G	A	I	R	T
D	K	S	L	A	I	E	T	W	D	A	L	U	N	O
O	E	A	V	P	R	A	N	A	K	R	N	M	S	T
O	K	E	E	F	R	S	P	O	R	D	N	I	A	R
W	S	E	A	S	E	L	C	A	A	E	O	O	M	M
N	L	L	R	I	S	O	S	A	W	N	A	V	W	E
S	L	E	K	O	M	S	E	S	N	E	C	N	I	G

AQUARIUM	SLEEPING ANIMALS
CANDLE	SNOW
FALLING LEAVES	STARS
INCENSE SMOKE	STREAM
KALEIDOSCOPE	SUNRISE
LAKE	SUNSET
LOG FIRE	WATERFALL
MEADOW	WAVES
RAINBOW	WOODLAND
RAINDROPS	ZEN GARDEN

Place all of the listed words into the grid, crossword-style.

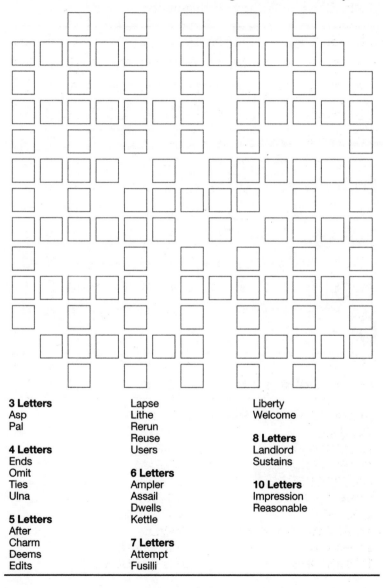

3 Letters
Asp
Pal

4 Letters
Ends
Omit
Ties
Ulna

5 Letters
After
Charm
Deems
Edits

Lapse
Lithe
Rerun
Reuse
Users

6 Letters
Ampler
Assail
Dwells
Kettle

7 Letters
Attempt
Fusilli

Liberty
Welcome

8 Letters
Landlord
Sustains

10 Letters
Impression
Reasonable

Solve the clues to write a word on each row, one letter per block. Each row contains the same letters as the previous row, plus one extra letter – but the letters may be in a different order.

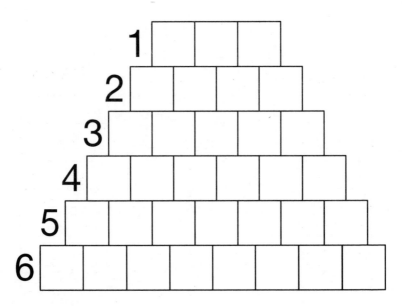

1. Space

2. Surprised breath

3. Stares

4. Wine source

5. Understood

6. Improvements

Rearrange these boxes to spell out five **natural water features**. Each box will be used exactly once.

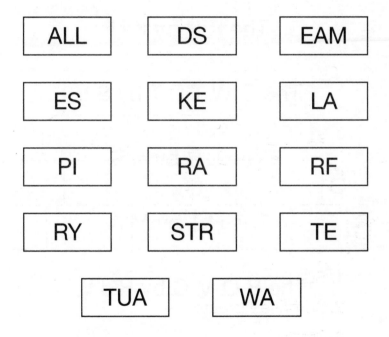

Can you identify all five of the following **novels beginning with 'The'**, for which otherwise only the initial letters of their titles are given? The initials of the novel's author are also given.

The K R by K H

The G W T D T by S L

The L B by A S

The H T by M A

The B O M C by R J W

For each line, find a word of the indicated length that can both join to the end of the preceding word to make a new word, and join to the start of the following word to make a new word. For example, OUT _ _ _ _ LED could be joined with GROW to make OUTGROW and GROWLED.

LIVE _ _ _ _ _ MARKET

UP _ _ _ _ _ RALLY

ARC _ _ _ SELF

SIDE _ _ _ _ DOWN

OVER _ _ _ _ HELL

Find all these **bones of the body** in the grid in any direction. The middle of the grid has been hidden, however, and it is up to you to identify these 25 missing letters.

L	D	A	S	E	A	V	E	S	A	L	U	B	I	F
A	B	E	N	O	B	R	A	L	L	O	C	F	T	B
S	T	D	P	E	L	V	I	S	A	S	A	R	T	F
R	O	P	H	A	L	A	N	G	E	S	A	L	E	A
A	M	M	S	A	F	F	T	M	A	P	A	N	D	L
T	V	E	M	T						B	O	T	Z	L
A	E	I	T	M						B	U	E	R	E
T	R	C	U	A						R	L	A	M	T
E	T	R	A	E						B	E	E	S	A
M	E	S	T	R						A	B	M	M	P
E	B	S	U	U	P	E	R	D	B	I	L	I	U	S
O	R	K	A	L	R	U	N	P	B	O	N	E	V	H
P	A	U	A	B	N	A	S	R	A	N	N	P	E	C
T	C	L	T	E	M	P	O	R	A	L	S	E	A	B
P	T	L	U	N	A	E	L	I	R	A	D	I	U	S

BREASTBONE	PATELLA
CARPUS	PELVIS
COLLARBONE	PHALANGES
FEMUR	RADIUS
FIBULA	SKULL
FRONTAL	STERNUM
HUMERUS	TAILBONE
MANDIBLE	TEMPORAL
METACARPAL	TRAPEZIUM
METATARSAL	VERTEBRA

Time: _____

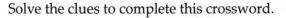

Solve the clues to complete this crossword.

Across
1 Twine (6)
5 Reason out (6)
8 Clenched hand (4)
9 Freedom from external control (8)
10 Chaos (8)
11 Animal flesh eaten as food (4)
12 Type of TV (6)
14 Live in (6)
16 List of options (4)
18 Protecting (8)
20 Wedding paper scraps (8)
21 Basic part of speech (4)
22 Dispatcher (6)
23 Nominating (6)

Down
2 Insignificant (7)
3 Opening (5)
4 Child's female child (13)
5 Decay (13)
6 Energetic (7)
7 A certain punctuation mark (5)
13 Full up (7)
15 Flightless seabird (7)
17 Abscond with a lover (5)
19 Jeans fabric (5)

Crack the letter-shift code in order to identify five **moons of Jupiter**. The same code is used for all five lines. For example, 'A' might have become 'B'; 'B' might have become 'C'; and so on.

DXKVJBAB

QEBJFPQL

XAOXPQBX

QEBYB

FL

A	B	C	D	E	F	G	H	I	J	K	L	M

N	O	P	Q	R	S	T	U	V	W	X	Y	Z

Unscramble the following anagrammed '+1' words to reveal
five **types of fruit**. Each line has had **one extra letter added**,
however, which is not part of the anagram. Read all these
extracted letters in order from top-to-bottom to reveal a
sixth fruit. Ignore any spaces in the anagrams.

ARCHERY

PAN A NAB

ACHE PP

A LONGER

UP ELM

Time: _____

Can you solve this cryptic crossword?
For clue format help, see **en.wikipedia.org/wiki/Cryptic_crossword**

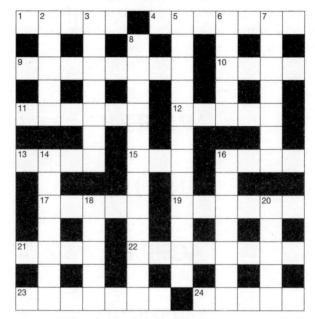

Across

1 Good lecturer given award in circle (5)
4 Pies Sam concocted in stalemate (7)
9 Popular profit as an exchange (2,6)
10 Insect hidden in clearing naturally (4)
11 Moderate means for broadcasting (6)
12 Something that can be attached, we hear, for a set of notes (5)
13 Postman typically by hospital walkway (4)
15 Have a short sleep in North American place principally (3)
16 Horrible-looking extremists in unprepossessing locality (4)
17 Pleasant scent in a foreign capital according to its residents (5)
19 Line followed by a court in charge regarding some acid? (6)
21 Correct part of scheduled itinerary (4)
22 Vaguely present like oxygen? (2,3,3)
23 Leading way to describe a member of a revolutionary group? (2,5)
24 Time that's left for ex-US president (5)

Down

2 Sudden thrust or dive concealing head (5)
3 Unsightly mark Miles developed in confines of bush (7)
5 Militancy up I fancy in city (12)
6 A Greek taking part in game in trouble (5)
7 Closely examine US lawyer left in disgrace (7)
8 Eating amount after analysis shows increase (12)
14 Leave a group in operation (7)
16 Male relative given a right? That's uncertain (7)
18 External computing device needing no introduction (5)
20 Mode of speech from inspector in the Isle of Man (5)

Can you identify all of the following **motivational words**, each of which has had all of its vowels deleted?

NCRG

BLV

MPWR

TTN

SCCD

Find the listed **shades of blue** written in the grid in any
direction, including diagonally. Some of the words 'wrap
around' the edges of the puzzle, continuing as if the puzzle
repeated edge-to-edge forever.

R	I	O	H	R	T	O	L	R	A
R	B	G	E	S	T	E	U	E	U
A	I	D	E	E	E	S	S	Z	I
N	W	P	E	R	S	I	A	N	L
O	S	R	O	I	I	C	N	T	D
K	Y	Y	A	P	O	Y	S	I	P
V	A	N	O	H	U	A	M	U	Y
L	U	R	E	C	Q	N	N	A	E
P	P	A	S	Y	R	E	R	I	H
R	E	S	C	T	U	K	N	N	P

AZURE	NAVY
CERULEAN	PERSIAN
COBALT	POWDER
CYAN	PRUSSIAN
ETON	ROYAL
IRIS	SAPPHIRE
KLEIN	SKY
MIDNIGHT	TURQUOISE

In this coded crossword, every letter has been replaced by a number. Each number represents a different letter of the alphabet. Crack the code to complete the crossword.

	19		26		9		23		18		22
13	2	10	17	13	23		11	3	13	22	21
	26		13		10	5	23		20		26
12	10	7	19	26	24			5	26	20	3	5
26			16				18		14 **P**		11	
18	23 **E**	9	10	23	15		26	5	23	2	26
19		23			3	24	9 **L**			23		10
	18	26	19	10	2		9	23	11	23	9	19
	23		3		25				10			9
24	23	23	2	4			21	13	6	26	2	23
10		11		3	26	25		1		11	
19	13	10	2	7		13	25	3	14	10	26
21		9		26		8		2		1	

1	2	3	4	5	6	7	8	9	10	11	12	13
14	15	16	17	18	19	20	21	22	23	24	25	26

A B C D E F G H I J K L M N O P Q R S T U V W X Y Z

Write a letter in each shaded square, to form seven words.
The last two letters of each word form the first two letters of
the following word, in the same order, as indicated by the
shaded lines.

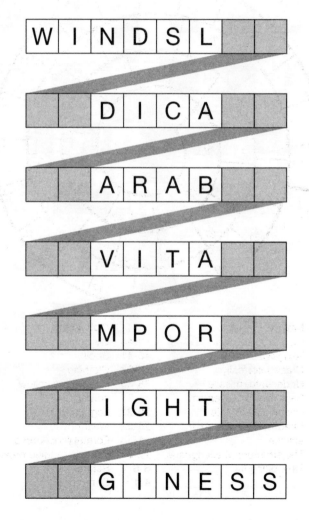

W	I	N	D	S	L		

		D	I	C	A		

		A	R	A	B		

		V	I	T	A		

		M	P	O	R		

		I	G	H	T		

		G	I	N	E	S	S

Each letter in this spiral crossword is clued twice: once reading inwards, and once reading outwards.

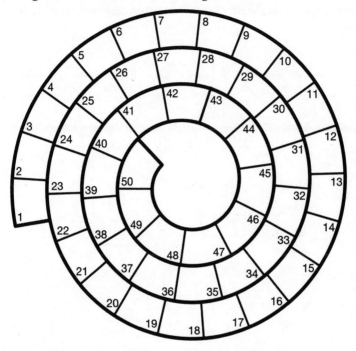

Inward

1-6	Medieval restraints
7-13	Text revisers
14-17	Crazy, informally
18-24	Underwater missile
25-30	Best-ever achievement
31-34	Despicable people
35-39	Shadow seen during an eclipse
40-46	The structure of a language
47-50	Tiny, biting fly

Outward

50-44	Cut-paper puzzle
43-41	Spoil
40-37	Clothing
36-30	Hot-tasting yellow condiment
29-27	Legendary bird
26-22	Wear down
21-13	Formal procedures
12-9	Round, griddled bread
8-5	School table
4-1	Camp beds

Can you find the word '**SPIDER**' in this network? Start on any circle and then follow lines to touching circles, spelling out the word circle by circle. No circle can be revisited.

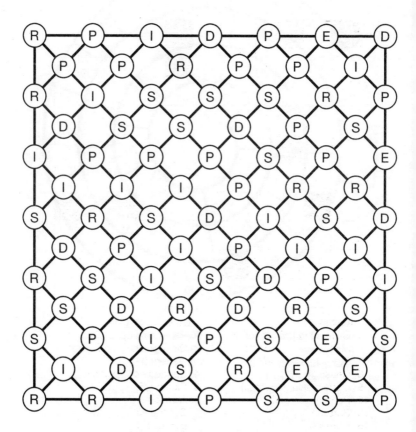

To complete this crossword you must not only solve the clues but also add the missing shaded squares and clue numbers to the grid. The shading has rotational symmetry.

Across
1 Orders the production of (11)
7 Big-screen venue (6)
8 Cease (4)
9 Certain skin growth (4)
10 Personal account (6)
13 Surroundings (6)
16 Cheek (4)
17 Fetches (4)
18 Made tea (6)
19 Focus (11)

Down
2 Paper-folding art (7)
3 Distinguished orchestral leaders (7)
4 Sudden convulsion (5)
5 Exceed (5)
6 Awesome (5)
11 Get the wrong idea, perhaps (7)
12 Look at closely (7)
13 Prestidigitation (5)
14 Ancient Roman language (5)
15 In a town or city (5)

Link the top word to the bottom word by writing a word on each step, changing just one letter at a time while also possibly rearranging the letters. For example, you could change CAT to COT, then to DOT and finally to DOG.

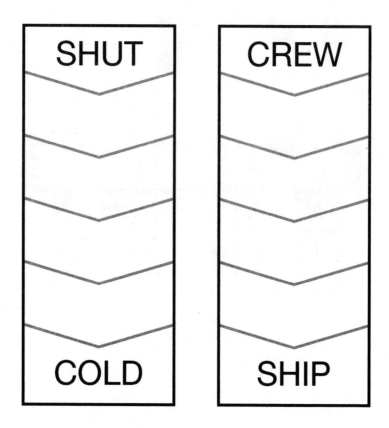

SHUT

COLD

CREW

SHIP

How many different five-letter words can you spell using this word slider? Imagine sliding each of the tabs up and down to reveal different letters through the central window. One word is spelled already.

Target:
10 words

Find the listed words **all related to education** written in the grid in any direction, including diagonally.

```
P  L  A  O  R  U  N  I  V  E  R  S  I  T  Y
E  M  G  N  I  N  R  A  E  L  S  O  N  E  N
D  M  E  G  E  L  L  O  C  C  K  E  U  E  O
A  U  Y  R  A  C  D  L  O  O  M  T  N  R  I
G  L  D  S  S  C  O  U  O  S  E  O  T  E  T
O  U  U  O  E  O  R  B  S  A  S  E  L  H  I
G  C  T  R  H  S  T  E  C  S  A  C  C  T  U
Y  I  S  C  E  X  S  H  E  C  A  R  S  T  T
A  R  S  R  E  S  E  L  E  G  A  S  L  C  X
A  R  L  T  A  R  O  E  U  E  O  T  L  E  L
H  U  E  M  O  O  R  S  S  A  L  C  I  J  G
Y  C  E  L  A  K  S  E  M  A  X  E  K  O  T
A  M  S  L  S  N  R  I  H  C  U  S  S  R  S
L  E  Q  U  E  S  T  I  O  N  S  E  N  P  S
L  N  L  I  V  V  E  G  D  E  L  W  O  N  K
```

ASSESSMENT	PROJECT
CLASSROOM	QUESTIONS
COLLEGE	RESEARCH
COURSE	SCHOOL
CURRICULUM	SKILLS
EXAM	STUDY
KNOWLEDGE	TEACHER
LEARNING	TEXTBOOK
LESSON	TUITION
PEDAGOGY	UNIVERSITY

Place all of the listed words into the grid, crossword-style.

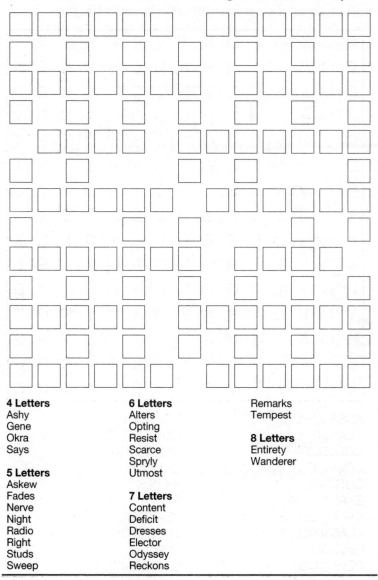

4 Letters
Ashy
Gene
Okra
Says

5 Letters
Askew
Fades
Nerve
Night
Radio
Right
Studs
Sweep

6 Letters
Alters
Opting
Resist
Scarce
Spryly
Utmost

7 Letters
Content
Deficit
Dresses
Elector
Odyssey
Reckons

Remarks
Tempest

8 Letters
Entirety
Wanderer

Solve the clues to write a word on each row, one letter per block. Each row contains the same letters as the previous row, plus one extra letter – but the letters may be in a different order.

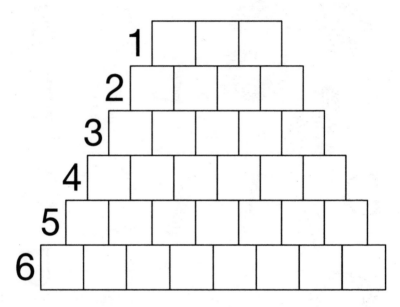

1. Old cloth

2. Rugged cliff

3. Elegance

4. More reticent

5. Ice river

6. Intolerant

Can you rearrange these letters to reveal four **jobs**? Each
letter will be used exactly once, with no letters left over.

How many words can you form that use the middle letter plus two or more of the other letters? No letter may be used more times than it appears within the circle. There is one word that uses all nine letters.

Target:
50 words

For each line, find a word of the indicated length that can both join to the end of the preceding word to make a new word, and join to the start of the following word to make a new word. For example, OUT _ _ _ _ LED could be joined with GROW to make OUTGROW and GROWLED.

IMP _ _ _ WORK

WHIRL _ _ _ _ SWEPT

STAG _ _ _ _ _ _ ALLY

LANDS _ _ _ _ RED

MINI _ _ _ BLED

Find the listed words **zigzagging through the grid**, in any direction. Each word zigs and zags after every letter, as shown by the example highlighted word.

N	G	T	E	N	N	D	K	U	N	G	W	N	H	D
D	P	S	E	S	I	A	E	I	A	G	E	N	T	N
N	S	R	G	N	S	I	R	O	E	P	T	D	N	D
L	I	R	C	I	D	E	W	P	T	N	I	I	E	E
T	M	I	N	N	I	S	A	E	A	E	S	R	V
E	P	R	D	R	G	W	E	W	I	N	G	R	R	S
D	R	U	D	N	T	I	A	E	R	I	S	E	T	U
S	R	T	S	D	I	E	V	D	E	A	N	E	C	R
S	W	D	R	G	E	D	A	N	E	E	N	E	A	S
D	T	I	E	L	R	M	E	C	Y	E	D	I	U	G
E	S	N	E	E	K	S	W	D	E	E	N	U	G	O
D	R	T	R	N	V	U	E	R	D	A	I	R	U	L
R	E	U	E	I	I	E	W	V	I	E	R	V	Y	N
V	R	D	T	R	D	V	N	P	N	G	H	T	I	E
M	N	R	G	E	C	K	I	E	N	D	T	D	V	S

CRIMPED	STRAGGLY
CRINKLED	SWERVING
CURVED	THREADED
DIVERGING	TURNED
MEANDERING	TWISTED
SERPENTINE	WEAVED
SINUOUS	WEND
SNAKING	WINDING

Time: _____

Solve the clues to complete this crossword.

Across

1 Declare (5)
4 Successfully opposes (7)
9 Side by side (8)
10 Freezes over (4)
11 Rich, moist cake (6)
12 Kitchen frothing device (5)
13 Kids' spotting game (1,3)
15 With frozen water (3)
16 Rows a boat (4)
17 Subsidiary theorem in a proof (5)
19 Uncouth (6)
21 Maned cat (4)
22 Engrave (8)
23 Deleting (7)
24 Absolutely love (5)

Down

2 Ornamental headgear (5)
3 Dramatic genre (7)
5 Rehabilitation venue (7,5)
6 Proof of being elsewhere (5)
7 Hiker (7)
8 Light (12)
14 Wackier (7)
16 Proposed (7)
18 Less (5)
20 Not drunk (5)

Time: _____

Find a hidden five-letter word, based on the mildly cryptic clue. Four incorrect guesses have already been made, and the individual letters in each guess marked as either:

- Correct, and in the right position, marked in black
- Correct, but in the wrong position, marked in grey
- Not in the word, marked with a white background

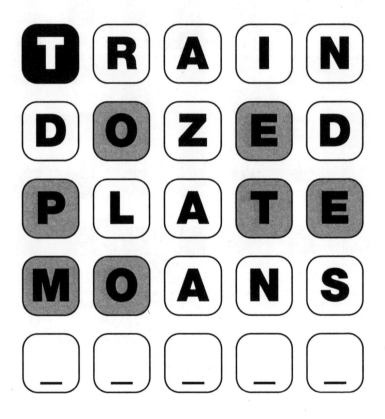

Clue: It's about time

WORD GAME 90 Time: __________

Delete one letter from each of the pairs below to reveal five hidden words.

TD RU ES ED

SD OR EL VA MG

SC AW ER BA RO LN

FB IE GN OI SN HI AE

PD IE SC TU NR AI AC TR IY

Solve this crossword which has all of its clues written within the grid.

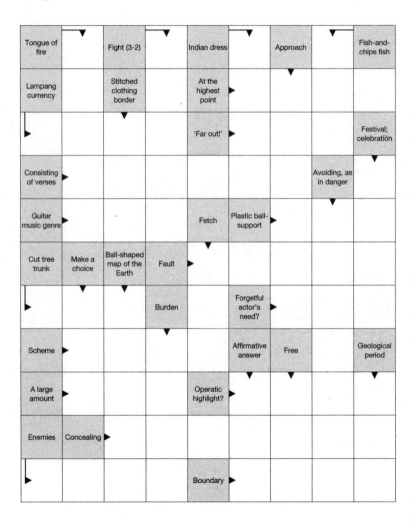

Tongue of fire	▼	Fight (3-2)	▼	Indian dress	▼	Approach	▼	Fish-and-chips fish
Lampang currency		Stitched clothing border		At the highest point ▶	▼			
▶		▼		'Far out!' ▶				Festival; celebration
Consisting of verses ▶							Avoiding, as in danger	▼
Guitar music genre ▶				Fetch	Plastic ball-support ▶	▼		
Cut tree trunk	Make a choice	Ball-shaped map of the Earth	Fault ▶	▼				
▶	▼	▼	Burden		Forgetful actor's need? ▶			
Scheme ▶			▼	Affirmative answer	Free		Geological period
A large amount ▶			Operatic highlight? ▶	▼	▼		▼
Enemies	Concealing ▶						
▶			Boundary ▶				

Each of the following words is missing its first and last letter, which must – for each word – be identical. For example, _XAMPL_ could be solved with 'E', to give 'EXAMPLE'.

_EX_

_OB_

EFEN

INU

_LS_

Can you find an **animal** hidden within all of the following phrases? Each animal must have at least four letters, and will be formed of continuous letters. For example, 'Please decode most of them' contains 'demo', as highlighted.

1. Over such a long timespan there have been many different animals evolve

2. On my last visit to the barber, right in the middle of my scalp, a careless mistake led to an accidental bald patch

3. The music hurtled through so many different tempos, summarizing its pace was extremely tricky

4. When we reached the central proposal, a man derailed all of the previously agreed settlements

5. I stood in awe as elaborate scenes unfolded on the big screen, right in front of my eyes

Find the listed **shades of green** written in the grid in any direction, including diagonally. Some of the words 'wrap around' the edges of the puzzle, continuing as if the puzzle repeated edge-to-edge forever.

```
E  L  T  R  Y  M  A  E  G  J
C  C  E  L  A  D  O  N  L  U
S  P  O  L  I  V  E  M  R  P
P  E  R  F  E  R  N  F  I  O
C  A  A  L  A  E  T  O  E  N
T  R  S  S  M  I  E  R  A  P
I  S  S  L  P  R  S  E  L  O
A  R  E  M  E  A  A  S  D  L
P  D  L  V  A  M  R  T  O  R
A  R  O  L  I  M  E  A  G  M
```

APPLE	JADE
ASPARAGUS	LIME
CELADON	MINT
CLOVER	MOSS
EMERALD	MYRTLE
FERN	OLIVE
FOREST	PEAR
GRASS	TEAL

Time: _____

In this coded crossword, every letter has been replaced by a number. Each number represents a different letter of the alphabet. Crack the code to complete the crossword.

19	21	8	3	15		16	18	11	24	2	8	19
	2		22		16 **E**		11		2		16	
15	8	16	22	11	17	16	19		15	3	26	16
	9		3		4		21		3		11	
14	11	5	11	23	11		2	2	25	16	19 **S**	
			8		7		23				16	
11	8	11	19		3	21	24		1	16	19	24
	16				8		11		2			
	10	20	2	24	3		23	3	11	26	16	8
	20		23		24		20		23		23	
5	11	13	11		11	18	16	23	24	11	24	12
	8		2		23		18		7		16	
24	16	16	23	3	9	16		6	12	8	8 **R**	4

1	2	3	4	5	6	7	8	9	10	11	12	13
14	15	16	17	18	19	20	21	22	23	24	25	26

A B C D E F G H I J K L M N O P Q R S T U V W X Y Z

Write a letter in each shaded square, to form seven words. The last two letters of each word form the first two letters of the following word, in the same order, as indicated by the shaded lines.

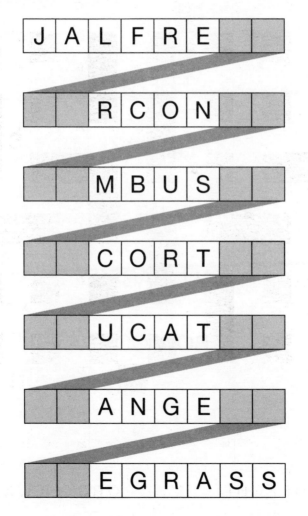

J	A	L	F	R	E		
		R	C	O	N		
		M	B	U	S		
		C	O	R	T		
		U	C	A	T		
		A	N	G	E		
		E	G	R	A	S	S

Unscramble the following anagrammed words to reveal five **types of hat**. Ignore any spaces or punctuation.

EBERT

LIB TRY

DO, RE, FA

ALL BABES

BOW COY

Find as many words as you can by starting on any letter and
tracing a path to touching squares, including diagonally
touching squares. Do not revisit any square within a word.
There is one word that uses all of the letters.

Y	A	L
L	R	I
S	I	M

Target:
20 words

Half of the letters have been deleted from each of the following words. Can you restore them in order to reveal five **rainforests**?

_O_G_   _I_E_   _A_I

A_A_O_I_

H_W_I_A_

_L_M_I_

B_R_E_   _O_L_N_

See how quickly you can complete this smaller, break-time crossword.

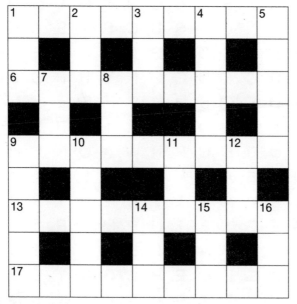

Across
1 Shortened (9)
6 Preoccupation (9)
9 Sparkling wine (9)
13 Threatening, in chess (9)
17 Ridiculously (9)

Down
1 Moreover (3)
2 Hikes; raises (3)
3 Type of lettuce (3)
4 Entity (5)

5 Not very clever (5)
7 'Harrumph!' (3)
8 Tree with rough, serrated leaves (3)
9 Trainer (5)
10 Performed (5)
11 Put a question to (3)
12 Convent dweller (3)
14 Pigeon sound (3)
15 Maybes (3)
16 Bloke (3)

Time: _____

Find the listed **herbal teas** written in the grid in any direction, including diagonally.

```
P  P  N  S  S  A  R  G  N  O  M  E  L  N  R
O  L  I  N  U  R  S  U  C  S  I  B  I  H  R
A  E  K  H  R  O  S  G  E  S  A  G  E  O  E
Y  I  R  C  E  O  G  O  N  Y  R  R  S  E  G
E  E  O  E  O  S  H  M  B  Y  R  E  J  M  N
N  L  L  H  L  D  O  T  R  I  M  R  G  Y  I
O  G  D  R  E  C  R  R  W  A  O  H  E  H  G
M  N  L  E  A  R  E  U  R  A  E  O  I  T  D
A  E  E  U  R  B  T  Y  B  E  H  I  R  R  N
N  S  E  R  I  B  T  U  R  M  E  R  I  C  A
N  N  T  J  F  A  E  L  E  L  T  T  E  N  N
I  I  O  G  E  M  E  R  E  G  N  Y  E  O  O
C  G  N  C  E  T  R  M  R  B  T  N  I  M  M
L  E  N  N  E  F  N  N  E  Y  S  M  S  S  E
R  E  G  I  N  G  E  R  R  O  O  T  A  Y  L
```

BARLEY	LEMON AND GINGER
BURDOCK	LEMONGRASS
CINNAMON	MINT
ELDERBERRY	NETTLE LEAF
FENNEL	ROOIBOS
GINGER ROOT	ROSE HIP
GINSENG	ROSEMARY
GOJI BERRY	SAGE
HAWTHORN	THYME
HIBISCUS	TURMERIC

Place all of the listed words into the grid, crossword-style.

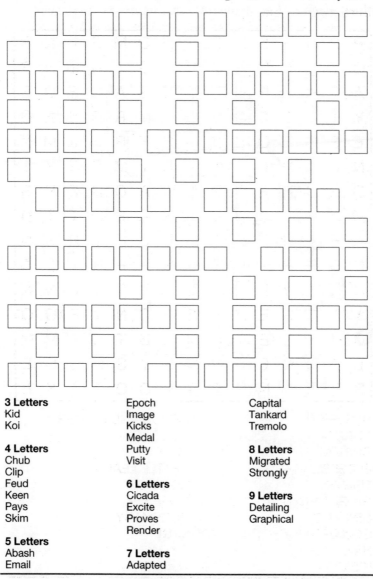

3 Letters
Kid
Koi

4 Letters
Chub
Clip
Feud
Keen
Pays
Skim

5 Letters
Abash
Email

Epoch
Image
Kicks
Medal
Putty
Visit

6 Letters
Cicada
Excite
Proves
Render

7 Letters
Adapted

Capital
Tankard
Tremolo

8 Letters
Migrated
Strongly

9 Letters
Detailing
Graphical

Solve the clues to write a word on each row, one letter per block. Each row contains the same letters as the previous row, plus one extra letter – but the letters may be in a different order.

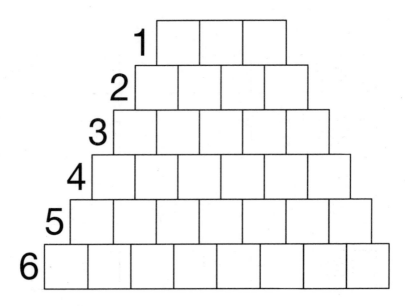

1. Droop

2. Catch

3. Swarming flies

4. Bursaries

5. Unusual

6. Police-officer ranking

Rearrange these boxes to spell out five **things you might need a ticket for**. Each box will be used exactly once.

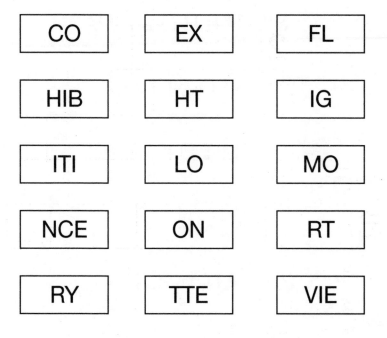

CO   EX   FL

HIB   HT   IG

ITI   LO   MO

NCE   ON   RT

RY   TTE   VIE

Can you identify all five of the following **chart hits by solo female vocal artists**, for which only the initial letters of their titles are given? The initial or initials of each artist are also given.

S L (P A R O I) by B

S I O by T S

R I T D by A

P F by L G

C M M by C R J

For each line, find a word of the indicated length that can both join to the end of the preceding word to make a new word, and join to the start of the following word to make a new word. For example, OUT _ _ _ _ LED could be joined with GROW to make OUTGROW and GROWLED.

FOOL   _ _ _ _ _   READ

BRAN   _ _ _ _   WASHER

MAN   _ _ _ _ _ _   BAR

WOOD   _ _ _ _   MILL

DAM   _ _ _ _   ION

Find all these **constellations** in the grid in any direction.
The middle of the grid has been hidden, however, and it is
up to you to identify these 25 missing letters.

H	R	A	H	C	A	H	S	R	S	U	C	V	C	S
C	C	C	D	A	A	U	E	I	I	A	J	I	Y	R
S	I	O	O	E	S	N	P	R	N	I	T	R	G	A
U	R	U	R	A	M	E	I	I	C	A	O	G	N	S
N	A	O	G	O	R	O	S	S	I	U	S	O	U	T
R	S	E	N	S						U	L	N	S	S
O	P	U	E	I						I	I	E	S	U
C	G	U	I	J						H	N	U	S	I
I	S	E	O	R						A	E	O	S	P
R	I	R	M	S						H	P	E	R	R
P	E	R	S	I	N	U	E	R	P	E	T	U	M	O
A	R	A	D	E	N	D	Q	E	U	E	A	N	I	C
C	C	A	C	O	I	I	C	A	C	I	R	L	N	S
S	S	U	I	R	A	T	T	I	G	A	S	S	I	S
A	U	R	S	A	M	A	J	O	R	S	R	A	E	S

ANDROMEDA	DELPHINUS
AQUARIUS	GEMINI
CANIS MAJOR	HERCULES
CANIS MINOR	PEGASUS
CAPRICORNUS	PERSEUS
CASSIOPEIA	SAGITTARIUS
CENTAURUS	SCORPIUS
CEPHEUS	URSA MAJOR
CORONA BOREALIS	URSA MINOR
CYGNUS	VIRGO

Time: _____

Solve the clues to complete this crossword.

Across
1 Lack of concern (12)
8 Amber, eg (5)
9 Egg-shaped wind instrument (7)
10 Sailors (4)
11 The act of discarding (8)
14 Very young children (6)
15 Italian-style ice cream (6)
17 Generosity (8)
18 Lean (4)
20 Whirlwind (7)
22 Finish a meal (3,2)
23 Increase in velocity (12)

Down
1 Bad temper (12)
2 Someone giving a detailed account (9)
3 Soulful jazz genre (4)
4 From a distant place (6)
5 Illustrations (8)
6 Greek letter 'X' (3)
7 Writing tool (9,3)
12 Long, stringy pasta (9)
13 Create (8)
16 On land, not sea (6)
19 Sixth letter of the Greek alphabet (4)
21 Legendary bird (3)

Crack the letter-shift code in order to identify five **relatives**. The same code is used for all five lines. For example, 'A' might have become 'B'; 'B' might have become 'C'; and so on.

VGPCSBDIWTG

SPJVWITG

UPIWTG

CTEWTL

LXUT

A	B	C	D	E	F	G	H	I	J	K	L	M

N	O	P	Q	R	S	T	U	V	W	X	Y	Z

Unscramble the following anagrammed '+1' words to reveal five **types of fish**. Each line has had **one extra letter added**, however, which is not part of the anagram. Read all these extracted letters in order from top-to-bottom to reveal a sixth fish. Ignore any spaces in the anagrams.

FOLD PRUNE

CODE

ARC PR

SCRAP PEN

LASH NOM

Can you solve this cryptic crossword?

For clue format help, see **en.wikipedia.org/wiki/Cryptic_crossword**

Across

1 Erase slight mark (7)
5 Second fool is self-satisfied (4)
9 Previously substantial instance (7)
10 It helps to draw lines for one in a powerful position (5)
11 Prohibit Jack and Oscar getting stringed instrument (5)
12 Further note for all to see in training environment showing mineral (6)
14 Retired American fellow faces problem getting thing at end of a word? (6)
16 Some coupon chosen for South American garment (6)
18 Pay sadly put back on railway (6)
19 Daughter enthralled by exotic rice and alcoholic drink (5)
22 Economy that is for an attractive female (5)
23 On holiday, factory worker is rude (7)
24 Pleasant Mediterranean resort (4)
25 Empty place seen on film fringed by Scottish river (7)

Down

2 Martial arts actor touring India for a set of commercial outlets? (5)
3 Appear to mix having moved close (11)
4 Ministers from Cuba greatly affected with a time gone (6)
6 Snail, say, starts to move only loosely lately under summer conditions (7)
7 Clothing requiring arbitration in part (4)
8 Wordy bishop first in office inspired by poetic form (7)
10 Disapproving chap fouler when agitated about source of rebellion (11)
13 Rust shown by old posh car in fake exhibition initially (7)
15 Very busy work in craft (7)
17 Past bogeyman sadly putting out graduate (6)
20 Doctor given a paper or first version of document (5)
21 I study holy image (4)

Can you identify all of the following **types of reptile**, each of which has had all of its vowels deleted?

MNTR LZRD

GNT TRTS

GN

SNK

SKNK

Find the listed **shades of orange** written in the grid in any direction, including diagonally. Some of the words 'wrap around' the edges of the puzzle, continuing as if the puzzle repeated edge-to-edge forever.

```
S  L  R  N  A  I  S  R  E  P
R  M  I  L  I  O  N  T  V  E
Y  T  L  G  R  C  A  N  C  E
S  O  O  I  H  N  P  I  A  L
Y  P  B  M  G  T  R  K  R  O
H  U  A  E  A  T  I  P  R  R
R  C  R  N  E  T  C  M  O  A
B  I  A  A  I  L  O  U  T  N
N  A  R  E  R  S  T  P  E  G
L  O  N  A  P  A  H  D  M  E
```

ALLOY	PEACH
APRICOT	PERSIAN
BURNED	PUMPKIN
CARROT	SPANISH
CINNABAR	TANGERINE
LIGHT	TEA ROSE
MELON	TOMATO
ORANGE PEEL	VERMILION

Time: _____

In this coded crossword, every letter has been replaced by a number. Each number represents a different letter of the alphabet. Crack the code to complete the crossword.

	15 P	7	16	19	3	9	19		5	6	18	6
12		8		23		4		8		13		20
6	21	21	6	2	10	16		1	17 O	6	19	1
4		1		19		3 I		16		10		8
4	7	16	24	8		20	23	24	2	8	4	
3				14		26		17		6		26
17	23	1	15	23	1		9	10	17	19	8	4
4		4		8		6		17				6
	8	6	4	20	8	22		26	10	8	6	20
19		18		1		25		3		11		22
9	4	6	12	10		23	20	9	10	6	19	15
6		3		16		19		6		9		6
4	17	10	10		23	1	3	10	3	1	16	

1	2	3	4	5	6	7	8	9	10	11	12	13
14	15	16	17	18	19	20	21	22	23	24	25	26

A B C D E F G H I J K L M N O P Q R S T U V W X Y Z

Time: _____

Write a letter in each shaded square, to form seven words. The last two letters of each word form the first two letters of the following word, in the same order, as indicated by the shaded lines.

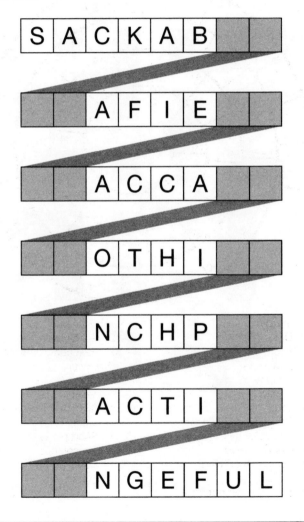

| S | A | C | K | A | B | | |

| | | A | F | I | E | | |

| | | A | C | C | A | | |

| | | O | T | H | I | | |

| | | N | C | H | P | | |

| | | A | C | T | I | | |

| | | N | G | E | F | U | L |

Time: _____

Each letter in this spiral crossword is clued twice: once reading inwards, and once reading outwards.

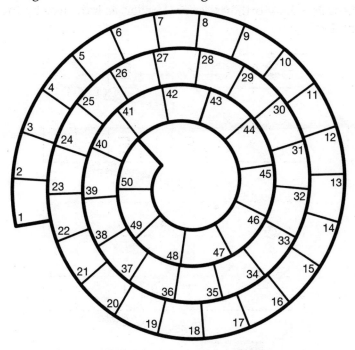

Inward

1-5	Upper classes
6-8	Food regurgitated by ruminants
9-12	Periphery
13-19	Foretell
20-23	Terse
24-28	Sample with the nose
29-33	Impulses
34-38	Hopping mad
39-42	On the other hand
43-45	Tit for ___
46-50	Stored a computer file

Outward

50-42	Wreak havoc on
41-37	Rain containing ice
36-32	Occur
31-27	Brusque
26-19	Teach
18-14	Alcoholic fermented-juice drink
13-11	Short pin or bolt
10-5	Reason out
4-1	Roofing slab

WORD GAME 117

Time: _____

Can you find the word '**CLUES**' in this network? Start on any circle and then follow lines to touching circles, spelling out the word circle by circle. No circle can be revisited.

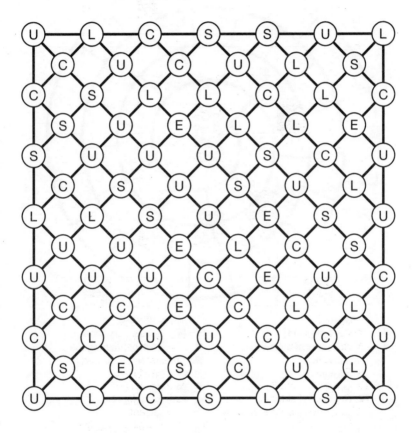

To complete this crossword you must not only solve the clues but also add the missing shaded squares and clue numbers to the grid. The shading has rotational symmetry.

Across

7 Viewpoint (11)
8 Culinary herb related to mint (7)
9 Female bird (3)
10 Letter after eta (5)
12 Respected elder (5)
13 Repeatedly bother or scold someone (3)
14 Distrustful (7)
16 Experts (11)

Down

1 Expediency (11)
2 Tall plant with a trunk (4)
3 Completely on-message official? (11)
4 As a result (11)
5 Fourscore (6)
6 Insignificant (11)
11 Large birds of prey (6)
15 Throw a fishing line (4)

Link the top word to the bottom word by writing a word on each step, changing just one letter at a time while also possibly rearranging the letters. For example, you could change CAT to COT, then to DOT and finally to DOG.

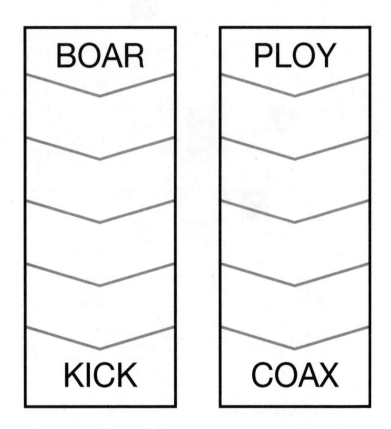

BOAR

KICK

PLOY

COAX

How many different five-letter words can you spell using this word slider? Imagine sliding each of the tabs up and down to reveal different letters through the central window. One word is spelled already.

Target:
15 words

WORD GAME 121

Time: _____

Find the listed words **related to feeling patient** written in the grid in any direction, including diagonally.

N	S	C	F	O	R	B	E	A	R	I	N	G	I	G
G	T	N	E	G	L	U	D	N	I	L	S	D	I	E
N	E	G	U	T	C	E	M	L	A	C	V	R	E	U
I	R	V	N	M	N	N	I	C	R	S	M	V	N	N
R	C	T	E	I	O	E	I	S	B	S	I	N	E	H
E	O	T	O	N	T	O	T	R	U	S	L	O	R	U
V	M	N	N	L	T	A	K	S	S	R	D	L	E	R
E	P	E	T	S	E	E	D	I	I	R	E	G	S	R
S	O	I	E	T	K	R	M	O	N	S	S	L	L	I
R	S	N	A	O	E	B	A	P	M	D	R	O	Y	E
E	E	E	B	T	U	E	F	N	E	M	E	E	L	D
P	D	L	N	S	R	N	E	F	T	R	O	I	P	N
S	E	G	N	I	O	G	Y	S	A	E	E	C	Y	E
O	O	F	O	R	G	I	V	I	N	G	E	D	C	O
G	A	L	L	D	E	N	I	A	R	T	S	E	R	A

ACCOMMODATING
CALM
COMPOSED
EASY-GOING
EVEN-TEMPERED
FORBEARING
FORGIVING
INDULGENT
KIND
LEISURELY

LENIENT
MILD
PERSEVERING
PERSISTENT
RESTRAINED
SERENE
STOICAL
SUBMISSIVE
TOLERANT
UNHURRIED

Place all of the listed words into the grid, crossword-style.

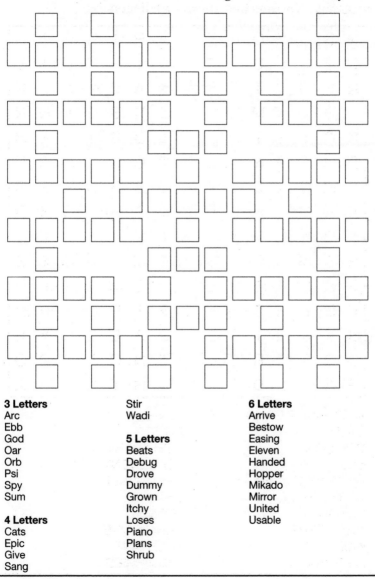

3 Letters	Stir	**6 Letters**
Arc	Wadi	Arrive
Ebb		Bestow
God	**5 Letters**	Easing
Oar	Beats	Eleven
Orb	Debug	Handed
Psi	Drove	Hopper
Spy	Dummy	Mikado
Sum	Grown	Mirror
	Itchy	United
4 Letters	Loses	Usable
Cats	Piano	
Epic	Plans	
Give	Shrub	
Sang		

Solve the clues to write a word on each row, one letter per block. Each row contains the same letters as the previous row, plus one extra letter – but the letters may be in a different order.

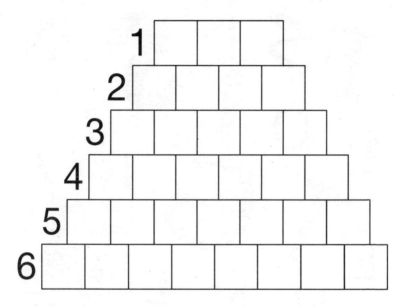

1. Label

2. Style of walking

3. Enormous

4. Consuming

5. Harnessing together

6. Attractive

Can you rearrange these letters to reveal four **sports**? Each letter will be used exactly once, with no letters left over.

Time: _____

How many words can you form that use the middle letter plus two or more of the other letters? No letter may be used more times than it appears within the circle. There is one word that uses all nine letters.

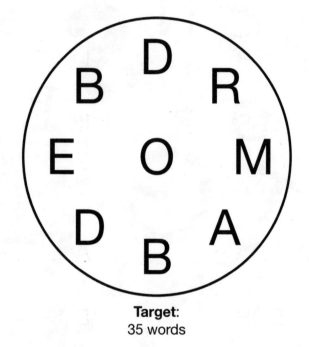

Target:
35 words

For each line, find a word of the indicated length that can both join to the end of the preceding word to make a new word, and join to the start of the following word to make a new word. For example, OUT _ _ _ _ LED could be joined with GROW to make OUTGROW and GROWLED.

OVER _ _ _ _ _ LESS

EAR _ _ _ _ IN

DATA _ _ _ _ LINE

ALPHA _ _ _ _ _ _ _ ALLY

BOB _ _ _ BUG

Find the listed birds **flying in the shape of a bird**. Each word is placed symmetrically, as in the example, but may read either from left to right or from right to left.

O	R	E	B	R	E	A	M	O	O	A	R	L	L	P
Y	I	I	O	G	R	I	P	M	W	R	L	R	O	K
O	R	W	A	I	N	O	W	S	U	O	L	E	K	W
D	R	K	P	H	R	S	M	O	N	H	R	O	H	M
C	H	W	G	P	O	R	O	N	I	G	P	A	R	S
S	S	W	E	P	I	O	D	B	A	L	T	U	I	E
L	E	R	S	I	O	P	N	W	N	S	L	N	N	L
O	I	E	N	O	W	G	A	A	L	L	T	R	O	A
E	R	G	H	U	U	E	N	L	R	T	M	O	O	R
H	T	P	A	N	T	T	R	O	A	O	C	G	T	C
O	M	W	C	S	I	E	W	C	N	O	G	H	R	A
M	U	H	Y	R	O	F	L	T	L	S	E	N	E	K
N	P	O	I	O	O	O	U	D	L	R	A	S	A	R
U	T	N	R	B	G	R	A	T	C	U	P	O	T	F
S	S	O	R	K	E	G	T	L	N	H	V	I	G	T

CORMORANT

GOLDCREST

GOOSE

HERON

HUMMINGBIRD

LAPWING

OYSTERCATCHER

ROBIN

SANDPIPER

SNOWFINCH

SPARROW

SPOONBILL

STORK

SWALLOW

VULTURE

WAGTAIL

Solve the clues to complete this crossword.

Across
1 A wish that is unlikely to come true (7,4)
9 Ambitious and go-getting (4-9)
10 Summation (8)
12 Circular-based geometric solid (4)
14 Employing (5)
15 Distasteful riches (5)
19 Walk through water (4)
20 Typesetting error (8)
22 Involving dramatic change (13)
24 Abolition (11)

Down
2 Canola or olive, eg (3)
3 Restricting (8)
4 Quantitative relations (6)
5 Possess (4)
6 Dried petal mix (9)
7 Regular (5)
8 Boundaries (5)
11 Small whirlwind (4,5)
13 'Straight away!' (4,2,2)
16 Stretch of short grass (5)
17 Fingerless glove (6)
18 Remains (5)
21 Dejected (4)
23 *Much ___ About Nothing* (3)

Find a hidden five-letter word, based on the mildly cryptic clue. Four incorrect guesses have already been made, and the individual letters in each guess marked as either:

- Correct, and in the right position, marked in black
- Correct, but in the wrong position, marked in grey
- Not in the word, marked with a white background

Clue: With luck, you'll be this

Delete one letter from each of the pairs below to reveal five hidden words.

LN UA UD NG EG

BC RO SE MA RO ST

PD RI NL EC EM MS AT

CV RI BO CR AU TS IF EO NR

SP AE PR AE RL LA EV LE

Solve this crossword which has all of its clues written within the grid.

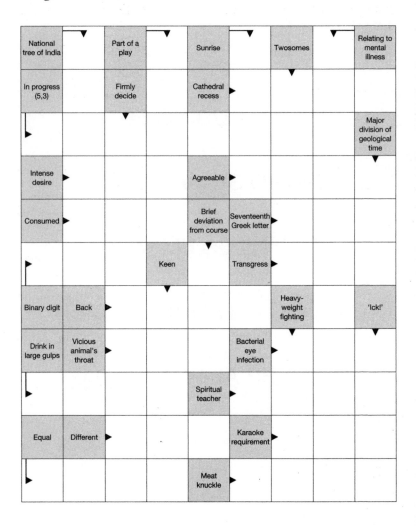

Each of the following words is missing its first and last letter, which must – for each word – be identical. For example, _XAMPL_ could be solved with 'E', to give 'EXAMPLE'.

YRI

_IT_

RYS

OWE

APE

Can you find a **vehicle** hidden within all of the following phrases? Each vehicle must have at least four letters, and will be formed of continuous letters. For example, 'Please deco<u>de mo</u>st of them' contains 'demo', as highlighted.

1. The bird trainer tricks hawks into flying only on command

2. High up in the air, the contrail erupted from the cloud like a bolt from the sky

3. The panel's ultimate conclusion was that they had been misled, generally, and the project should not proceed

4. As she began to rant, and emotions streamed across her face, she turned away from the camera

5. The day after the disco, aching limbs demonstrated his age more forcefully than the lines on his face

Find the listed **shades of white** written in the grid in any direction, including diagonally. Some of the words 'wrap around' the edges of the puzzle, continuing as if the puzzle repeated edge-to-edge forever.

```
C R E E M A R L E L
E L L R C S E A S H
W E I E B R K P A A
E O F A V A U L M I
L G N L T A B Y I N
E O G S A N N Y R S
N N N S B X O I P O
V R I G H E L T L O
W I O L A E I D T L
A D C C R M L G A O
```

BABY POWDER	IVORY
BEIGE	LINEN
CORNSILK	MAGNOLIA
COTTONTAIL	OLD LACE
CREAM	PEARL
ECRU	SEASHELL
EGGSHELL	SNOW
FLAX	VANILLA

Time: _____

In this coded crossword, every letter has been replaced by a number. Each number represents a different letter of the alphabet. Crack the code to complete the crossword.

6	18	19	21		8 **S**		8		17	8	7	8
18		21		10	21	23	1 **O**	15		16		13
9	20	17	19		25		15		10	17	20	21
21		16	1	5	13		17	12	17	20		10
	19		1		21	17	16		24		8	
12	17	9	22	17	14		17	4	21	15	16	8
	14			14				1			21	
17	14	22	17	14	18		8	1	14	6	21	10
	8		11		23	17	9		18		14	
21		14	18	8	7		1	26	14	8		14
19	18	1	8		21		20		2	1	22	21
19		5		8	15 **N**	17	9	22		19		26
8	18	16	21		10		3		13	8	21	10

1	2	3	4	5	6	7	8	9	10	11	12	13
14	15	16	17	18	19	20	21	22	23	24	25	26

A B C D E F G H I J K L M N O P Q R S T U V W X Y Z

Write a letter in each shaded square, to form seven words.
The last two letters of each word form the first two letters of
the following word, in the same order, as indicated by the
shaded lines.

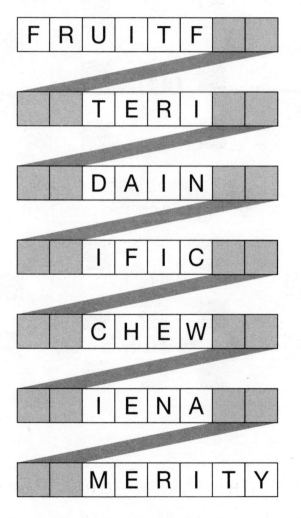

| F | R | U | I | T | F | | |

| | | T | E | R | I | | |

| | | D | A | I | N | | |

| | | I | F | I | C | | |

| | | C | H | E | W | | |

| | | I | E | N | A | | |

| | | M | E | R | I | T | Y |

Unscramble the following anagrammed words to reveal five **kitchen utensils**. Ignore any spaces.

BLOW

ELF NUN

CAN PAUSE

GRR TEA

HAREMS

Find as many words as you can by starting on any letter and tracing a path to touching squares, including diagonally touching squares. Do not revisit any square within a word. There is one word that uses all of the letters.

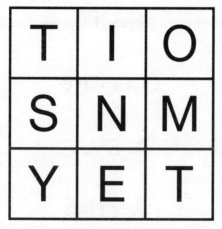

Target:
40 words

Half of the letters have been deleted from each of the following words. Can you restore them in order to reveal five **African animals**?

_I_A_F_

_O_G_O_E

_A_E_L_

_A_O_N

_E_U_

See how quickly you can complete this smaller, break-time crossword.

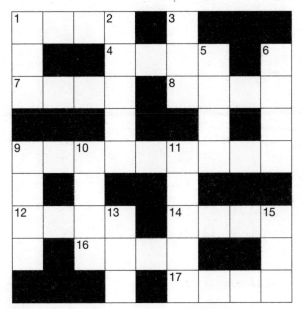

Across
1 Someone who looks down on others (4)
4 Mimics (4)
7 Military force (4)
8 Change from solid to liquid (4)
9 Fixing software (9)
12 Bovine animals (4)
14 Is behind on payment (4)
16 Former Italian currency unit (4)
17 Used in fluorescent lamps (4)

Down
1 Aegean, eg (3)
2 Marshy lake or river outlet (5)
3 Precious stone (3)
5 Penultimate match (4)
6 Male deer (4)
9 Tie a ship up (4)
10 Cry noisily (4)
11 Complain (5)
13 Computer emulation (3)
15 Largest star in the sky (3)

WORD GAME 141

Time: _____

Find the listed **rose cultivars** written in the grid in any direction, including diagonally.

```
K N N Y D G B E W I T C H E D
E I Y I H L L E H S A E S V H
H E N O R I A R E A E I N E Y
O L A T N A R V M V Y N U T K
T E F A R A T B N N A R R S S
C C F S R I E S D D O A U O Y
O T I L S R G N G P P N C O N
C R T O Q T A U E N F T F D N
O O I U E H R A E L I E O O U
A N E R A G N D A H D N R O S
T E C P A A R R I E O N E V C
N E S U C A E O N Y T D L V C
S I E N G C E E K A C P U C E
R D F R A N G E L F A C E O R
M O D N E C S E R C E F H L N
```

AMBER QUEEN
ANGEL FACE
BEWITCHED
CRESCENDO
CUPCAKE
EDEN
ELECTRON
ELINA
EUROPEANA
EVENING STAR

GARDEN PARTY
HOT COCOA
INTRIGUE
ISPAHAN
SEASHELL
SECRET
SUN FLARE
SUNNY SKY
TIFFANY
VOODOO

Place all of the listed words into the grid, crossword-style.

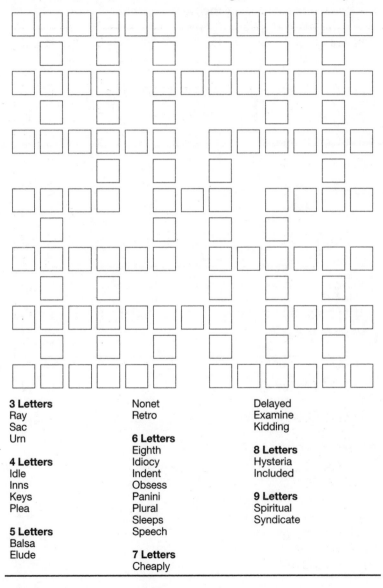

3 Letters
Ray
Sac
Urn

4 Letters
Idle
Inns
Keys
Plea

5 Letters
Balsa
Elude

Nonet
Retro

6 Letters
Eighth
Idiocy
Indent
Obsess
Panini
Plural
Sleeps
Speech

7 Letters
Cheaply

Delayed
Examine
Kidding

8 Letters
Hysteria
Included

9 Letters
Spiritual
Syndicate

Solve the clues to write a word on each row, one letter per block. Each row contains the same letters as the previous row, plus one extra letter – but the letters may be in a different order.

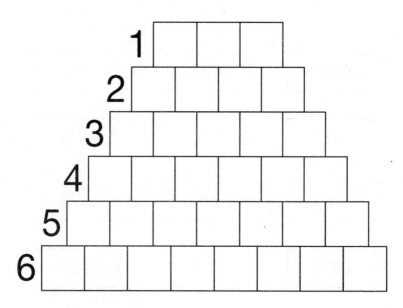

1. By way of

2. Narcissistic

3. Lacking experience

4. Seaborne military forces

5. Original residents

6. Certain years

Rearrange these boxes to spell out five **gardening tools**.
Each box will be used exactly once.

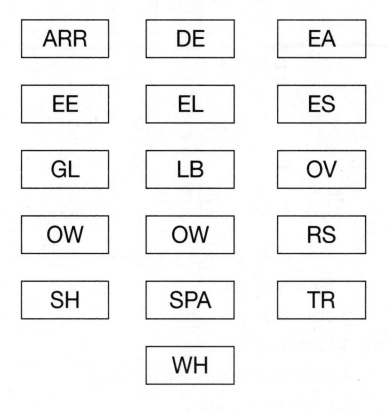

ARR	DE	EA
EE	EL	ES
GL	LB	OV
OW	OW	RS
SH	SPA	TR
	WH	

Can you identify all five of the following **bestselling video games**, all of which have a colon in their title, for which only the initial letters of their titles are given?

A C: N H

T L O Z: B O T W

C: S O T N

H: C E

S W: K O T O R

For each line, find a word of the indicated length that can both join to the end of the preceding word to make a new word, and join to the start of the following word to make a new word. For example, OUT _ _ _ _ LED could be joined with GROW to make OUTGROW and GROWLED.

SKY   _ _ _ _   STING

GRAPE   _ _ _ _ _   LESS

COMMIT   _ _ _   TOTAL

HOME   _ _ _ _ _   SHIP

HORSE   _ _ _ _   STRING

Find all these **African countries** in the grid in any direction.
The middle of the grid has been hidden, however, and it is
up to you to identify these 25 missing letters.

```
B C O B A Z S E N E G A L R R
A E N I U G Z E S A E A S R A
B U U N A R W S O U A T A E I
A V A A A B K M Q I I C A I N
A I P A A I U I T B S T N A A
U P B B A         E O I I T
B T M M A         O N N I I
I I D N A         F A I A R
Z A D Z S         Z A N N U
A A O I I         N A S I A
U M A Z M E A I A B H C N O M
D B E B I C A T B G O I D A A
C A P E V E R D E M M U I Z N
M A U R I T I U S T A A T O G
A N A W S T O B E E R Z E I S
```

BENIN	MAURITANIA
BOTSWANA	MAURITIUS
BURKINA FASO	MOZAMBIQUE
CAMEROON	NAMIBIA
CAPE VERDE	SENEGAL
DJIBOUTI	TANZANIA
GAMBIA	TUNISIA
GHANA	UGANDA
GUINEA	ZAMBIA
MADAGASCAR	ZIMBABWE

WORD GAME 148

Time: _____

Solve the clues to complete this crossword.

Across
- **7** Electorate (6)
- **8** Ceremonial fur (6)
- **9** Mid-month day (4)
- **10** Reply (8)
- **11** Revise (11)
- **14** Continue to fool (6,5)
- **18** Mad (8)
- **19** For hitting pool balls (4)
- **20** Fans (6)
- **21** Parentless child (6)

Down
- **1** Young child (7)
- **2** Checks out (4)
- **3** Hindu retreat (6)
- **4** Boat (6)
- **5** Everlasting (8)
- **6** Parsley relative (5)
- **12** Scandalized (8)
- **13** Openly mock (5,2)
- **15** Consume (6)
- **16** Male child sponsored at a baptism (6)
- **17** Extreme malice (5)
- **19** Handle a situation (4)

Crack the letter-shift code in order to identify five **things you might do in a yoga class**. The same code is used for all five lines. For example, 'A' might have become 'B'; 'B' might have become 'C'; and so on.

UMLQBIBQWV

MFMZKQAM

JITIVKM

NWKCA

XWAM

A	B	C	D	E	F	G	H	I	J	K	L	M

N	O	P	Q	R	S	T	U	V	W	X	Y	Z

Unscramble the following anagrammed '+1' words to reveal five **items of clothing**. Each line has had **one extra letter added**, however, which is not part of the anagram. Read all these extracted letters in order from top-to-bottom to reveal a sixth clothing item. Ignore any spaces in the anagrams.

SOB CLUE

LACK JET

S COOKS

IS TAU

DESK SR

Can you solve this cryptic crossword?
For clue format help, see **en.wikipedia.org/wiki/Cryptic_crossword**

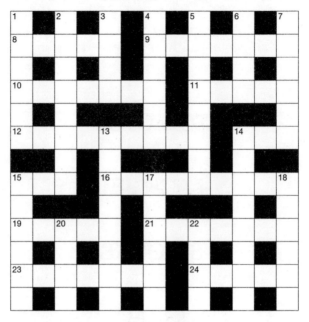

Across
8 Australian donated succulent plant (5)
9 Request for quiet by Tory unhappily interrupted by liberal in brief (7)
10 Making do somehow after leaving area in place with royal authority (7)
11 Time shown by start of this crafted poem (5)
12 I pour port mistakenly? A miscellany is required (9)
14 Cool supporter (3)
15 Moment, it's said, for nervous twitch (3)
16 Advice altered in deluge around India (9)
19 Recall river fringing good Scottish town (5)
21 Frenchman facing a trial sadly regarding relations with mate? (7)
23 Inhabitant gets to study independent Asian philosophy (7)
24 Some notes in bars? (5)

Down
1 Support returning at college (4,2)
2 Attractive gent possibly, one wearing waterproof coat (8)
3 A group of cattle, part of another drove (4)
4 Type of chemical compound a number of people found in Ireland (6)
5 Plan I convert at work (8)
6 Check part of a plant (4)
7 Magnate not coy for a change (6)
13 Arrange zero in a ground around start of game (8)
14 Most weak fellow replaced in state (8)
15 Hear about ambition that's fashionable (6)
17 Greek character put in working mine is exempt (6)
18 Intertwine new line kept by English expert (6)
20 Sticky material from weapon ending in trunk (4)
22 A light-hearted outing, a US high school ritual first to last (4)

Can you identify all of the following **arts and crafts**, each of which has had all of its vowels deleted?

RCHTCTR

MBRDRY

NMTN

RGM

MSC

Find the listed **shades of pink** written in the grid in any direction, including diagonally. Some of the words 'wrap around' the edges of the puzzle, continuing as if the puzzle repeated edge-to-edge forever.

```
L  D  I  O  E  B  B  U  A  H
A  K  H  U  S  B  A  N  T  A
C  N  A  L  O  L  B  A  M  N
O  R  A  G  R  E  Y  E  G  O
T  R  N  P  P  G  N  O  H  M
O  I  M  P  N  U  L  S  L  L
M  I  E  A  A  M  C  A  U  C
R  R  I  C  F  L  S  E  S  A
S  L  Y  A  G  B  E  I  L  H
U  C  N  N  T  U  N  F  S  I
```

BABY	PERSIAN
BUBBLEGUM	PUCE
CORAL	ROSE
CYCLAMEN	SALMON
FANDANGO	SHOCKING
FLAMINGO	SHRIMP
HOT	THULIAN
PALE	ULTRA

WORD GAME 154

Time: _____

In this coded crossword, every letter has been replaced by a number. Each number represents a different letter of the alphabet. Crack the code to complete the crossword.

	2		8		25		12		19		22	
17	6	21	26	25	6		9	21	6	22	9	11
	19		12		15		23		26 **I**		7	
10	26	18	21		5	23	11	26	18	26	7	18
	4				9		26		19		13	
6	11 **L**	6	4	15	17	26	4	26	15	13		
	6		17						6		26	
	16	9	6	21	15	26	5	7	26	7	18	
	6		21		13		25			2		
6	3	4	19	1	7	18	6		24	6	6	14
	12		26		15		1		6		17	
19	6	17	7	26	1		11	5	20	6	21	15 **T**
	11		18		3		21		11		6	

1	2	3	4	5	6	7	8	9	10	11	12	13
14	15	16	17	18	19	20	21	22	23	24	25	26

A B C D E F G H I J K L M N O P Q R S T U V W X Y Z

Write a letter in each shaded square, to form seven words.
The last two letters of each word form the first two letters of
the following word, in the same order, as indicated by the
shaded lines.

| B | R | A | S | S | I | | |

| | | L | E | N | D | | |

| | | B | O | R | E | | |

| | | K | A | L | I | | |

| | | C | K | L | A | | |

| | | L | E | R | I | | |

| | | C | E | D | I | N | G |

Each letter in this spiral crossword is clued twice: once reading inwards, and once reading outwards.

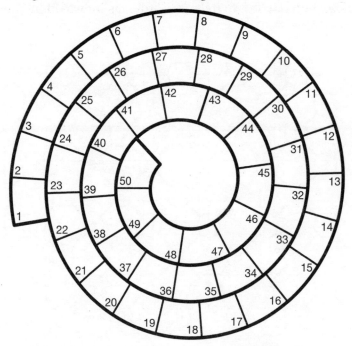

	Inward		**Outward**
1-7	Luggage	**50-47**	Loose soil or earth
8-11	Given birth to	**46-41**	Maintenance
12-18	Made possible	**40-34**	Human beings
19-23	Excludes	**33-26**	Felt curious about
24-30	Completed a purchase,		something
	perhaps	**25-21**	Swiss grated-potatoes dish
31-33	At once	**20-16**	Elle Macpherson, eg
34-37	Piece of blind	**15-13**	Prohibit
38-41	Frolic	**12-7**	Dress in vestments
42-44	'Oh my goodness!'	**6-4**	Mouth covering
45-50	Rotten; foul	**3-1**	Chatter

Can you find the word '**RECUR**' in this network? Start on any circle and then follow lines to touching circles, spelling out the word circle by circle. No circle can be revisited.

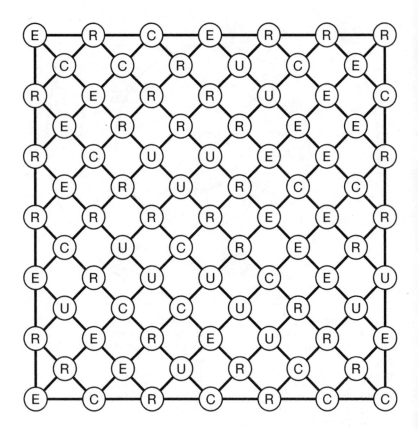

To complete this crossword you must not only solve the clues but also add the missing shaded squares and clue numbers to the grid. The shading has rotational symmetry.

Across
1 Overly complex administration (11)
7 Cling (6)
8 Wander around listlessly (4)
9 Book of maps (5)
11 Ill-suited (5)
13 Broad necktie (5)
14 Criminal (5)
16 Sleep resulting from trauma (4)
18 Complained (6)
20 Fortified places (11)

Down
2 Makes changes to (7)
3 It's surrounded by lashes (3)
4 Utilizes (4)
5 Courting (7)
6 It goes with a saucer (3)
10 Pear-shaped salad fruit (7)
12 Continue (7)
15 Haze (4)
17 Not in (3)
19 Back in time (3)

Link the top word to the bottom word by writing a word on each step, changing just one letter at a time while also possibly rearranging the letters. For example, you could change CAT to COT, then to DOT and finally to DOG.

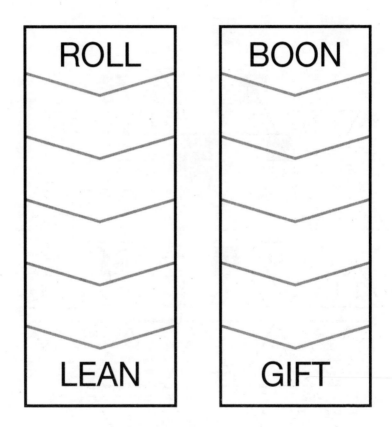

ROLL

LEAN

BOON

GIFT

Place all of the letter triangles into the grid, without rotating them, so that a word can be read across each of the six rows that are formed.

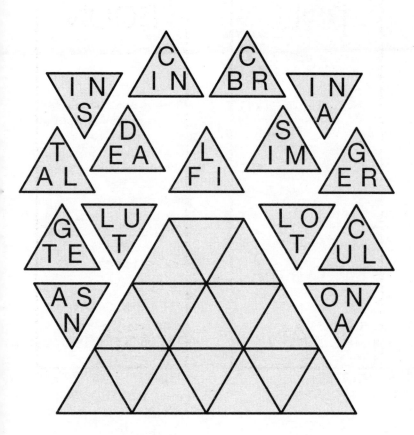

1.

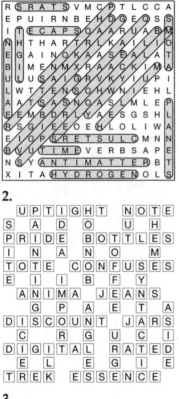

2.

```
  U P T I G H T     N O T E
S   A   D   O     U   H
P R I D E   B O T T L E S
I   N   A   N   O     M
T O T E   C O N F U S E S
E   I   I   B   F   Y
  A N I M A   J E A N S
  G   P   A   E   T   A
D I S C O U N T   J A R S
  C   R   G   U   C   I
D I G I T A L   R A T E D
  E   L   E   G   I   E
T R E K   E S S E N C E
```

3.
1. BAD
2. DABS
3. BASED
4. ABODES
5. BOASTED
6. BROADEST

4.
- ORCHID
- POPPY
- ROSE
- TULIP

5.
Words to find include chin, chins, chipmunk, **chipmunks**, chunk, chunks, cumin, hunk, hunks, inch, ink, inks, ins, kin, mink, minks, minus, munch, nick, nicks, nip, nips, pin, pinch, pink, pinks, pins, pun, punch, punish, punk, punks, puns, shin, shun, sin, sink, skin, snip, spin, spun, sun, sunk and unpick

6.
- READ: PROOFREAD and READJUST
- HERE: NOWHERE and HEREAFTER
- MASTER: POSTMASTER and MASTERPIECE
- CUR: CONCUR and CURTAIL
- BOW: CROSSBOW and BOWLED

7.

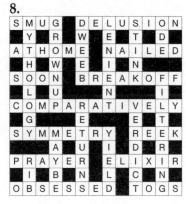

8.

```
S M U G ■ D E L U S I O N
■ Y ■ R ■ W E ■ T ■ D ■
A T H O M E ■ N A I L E D
■ H ■ W ■ E ■ I ■ N ■
S O O N ■ B R E A K O F F
■ L ■ U ■ N ■ ■ I ■
C O M P A R A T I V E L Y
■ G ■ E ■ ■ E ■ T ■
S Y M M E T R Y ■ R E E K
■ A ■ U ■ I ■ D ■ R ■
P R A Y E R ■ E L I X I R
■ I ■ B ■ N ■ L ■ C ■
O B S E S S E D ■ T O G S
```

9.
CRAZE

10.
- CLONE
- NINJA
- DRAGON
- PLATINUM
- COUNTERPOINT

11.

```
  N   E   S   O
  I   S   P I C K
A R T S   A N T
  V I A L   V A T
  A N Y   D I V A
  N   S   T E N
F A R   P E A
  E   I   T A G
A F F I X   I L L
  U   M I M O S A
G R A P E   N O D
```

12.
- SNORES
- ARMADA
- THEFT
- CHIC
- TAUT

13.
1. SPARROW: wa**sp, arrow**-like
2. ROBIN: heartth**rob in**
3. PIGEON: **pig, eon**s
4. STARLING: **star ling**ering
5. WREN: ne**w Ren**aissance

14.

15.

16.

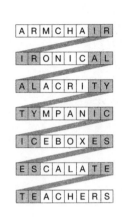

17.
- YAM
- ASPARAGUS
- ONION
- PARSNIP
- RADISH

18.
Words to find include aid, aide, air, ape, aped, arid, art, dear, depart, die, dip, dirt, ear, eat, edit, idea, paid, pair, par, part, partied, pat, patio, pea, pear, peat, pie, pied, pit, pita, raid, rap, rapid, rat, ratio, rid, ride, rip, ripe, tap, tape, taped, tapir, tar, taro, tide, tie, tied, tip, trap, **trapezoid**, tried, trio, trip, tripe and zip

SOLUTIONS

19.
- CROQUET
- TENNIS
- HOCKEY
- RUGBY
- BASEBALL

20.

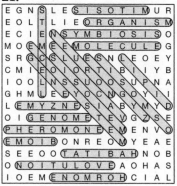

21.

22.

23.
1. TEA
2. TEAR
3. GREAT
4. GRATED
5. GRANTED
6. GRADIENT

24.
- GLUE
- ENVELOPE
- PENCIL
- RULER
- SCISSORS

25.
- Bill and Ted Face The Music
- Artemis Fowl
- Birds of Prey
- No Time to Die
- Sonic the Hedgehog

26.
- AGE: COINAGE and AGELONG
- HEM: MAYHEM and HEMLOCK
- LIME: SUBLIME and LIMELIGHT
- FRONT: FOREFRONT and FRONTAGE
- BACK: OUTBACK and BACKSLASH

27.

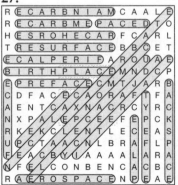

28.

29.
Decode by replacing A with E, B with F, C with G and so on through to replacing Y with C and Z with D:
- FERRIS WHEEL
- CAROUSEL
- CLOWN
- HAUNTED HOUSE
- ROLLER COASTER

30.
The sixth river is the INDUS:
- AMAZON + I
- NILE + N
- ORINOCO + D
- DANUBE + U
- RHINE + S

SOLUTIONS

31.

34.

32.

- AUSTRIAN AIRLINES (Austria)
- AIR PACIFIC (Fiji)
- ICELANDAIR (Iceland)
- ALITALIA (Italy)
- IBERIA (Spain)

35.

33.

36.

Inward: 1-5 PACKS; 6-12 ATTACKS; 13-18 ARISEN; 19-23 ROBOT; 24-28 SUGAR; 29-31 BEG; 32-36 LABEL; 37-42 ECLAIR; 43-45 ETA; 46-50 MEDIA. **Outward:** 50-47 AIDE; 46-39 MATERIAL; 38-34 CELEB; 33-27 ALGEBRA; 26-22 GUSTO; 21-17 BORNE; 16-14 SIR; 13-11 ASK; 10-8 CAT; 7-4 TASK; 3-1 CAP.

SOLUTIONS

37.

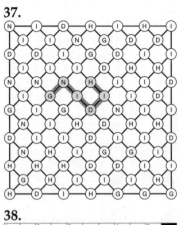

38.

P	O	L	I	T	E	N	E	S	S
A		A		I		R		I	
R	E	N	A	M	E		A	C	R	E
T		G		P		E		S	
R	H	U	B	A	R	B		N	A	P
I		A		N		U		T		I
D	I	G		I	N	F	E	R	N	O
G		E		F		A		N	
E	A	S	E		D	A	H	L	I	A
	R		G		L		L		G
	T	R	O	G	L	O	D	Y	T	E

40.

Words to find include drabs, dribs, drive, drove, glare, globe, globs, glove, grabs, grave, grove, share, shave, shire, shirt, shive, shivs, shore, short, shove, slabs, slave and slobs

41.

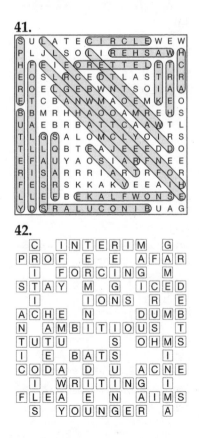

39.

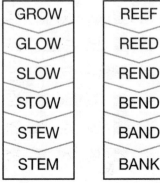

GROW / GLOW / SLOW / STOW / STEW / STEM

REEF / REED / REND / BEND / BAND / BANK

42.

C		I	N	T	E	R	I	M		G
P	R	O	F		E		E		A	F	A	R
I		F	O	R	C	I	N	G		M
S	T	A	Y		M		G		I	C	E	D
I			I	O	N	S		R		E
A	C	H	E		N			D	U	M	B
N		A	M	B	I	T	I	O	U	S		T
T	U	T	U			S		O	H	M	S
I		E		B	A	T	S			I
C	O	D	A		D		U		A	C	N	E
I		W	R	I	T	I	N	G		I
F	L	E	A		E		N		A	I	M	S
S		Y	O	U	N	G	E	R		A

43.
1. ATE
2. EAST
3. HASTE
4. BATHES
5. BREATHS
6. BRASHEST

44.
- FLUTE
- OBOE
- PIANO
- TRUMPET

45.
Words to find include across, also, carol, carols, carom, caroms, **classroom**, coal, coals, cols, coma, comas, coo, cool, cools, coos, coral, corals, corm, corms, cosmos, cross, loam, loco, loom, looms, loss, molar, molars, moo, moor, moors, moos, moral, morals, morass, moss, oar, oars, oral, orals, roam, roams, room, rooms, soar, soars, sol, solar, solo, solos and sols

46.
- BIRD: JAILBIRD and BIRDTABLE
- WAR: WARPATH and PATHWAY
- COT: MASCOT and COTTON
- RUST: MISTRUST and RUSTPROOF
- TOOL: FOOTSTOOL and TOOLBAR

47.

48.

O	F	F	S	E	T	S		B	O	O	S	T
	I		P		U		R		H		A	
E	N	T	E	R	T	A	I	N	M	E	N	T
	G		C		T		N				I	
D	E	S	I	R	I	N	G		R	O	T	S
	R		A				E		E		Y	
		C	L	O	S	E	D	O	W	N		
	F		L		C				R		B	
Q	U	A	Y		O	U	T	L	I	N	E	S
	L				F		A		T		M	
C	L	A	R	I	F	I	C	A	T	I	O	N
	U		Y		S		K		E		A	
U	P	P	E	R		A	S	I	N	I	N	E

49.
ADAGE

52.
- ENSURE
- DECKED
- LAUREL
- SHOES
- HURRAH

50.
- JEWEL
- LEOPARD
- CLEVER
- CITATION
- REVEALED

53.
1. ZINC: topa**z inc**luded
2. GOLD: Mon**gol d**ynasty
3. SILVER: uten**sil ver**y
4. BARIUM: sound**bar I um**bilically
5. IRON: cha**ir on**

51.

54.

55.

	S		R	E	Q	U	E	S	T		M	
D	A	T	A		U		M		A	K	I	N
	F		S	O	A	P	B	O	X		D	
L	A	M	P		N		E		I	B	I	S
	R			T	I	D	Y		E			H
R	I	F	E		U			E	R	G	O	
A		E	T	Y	M	O	L	O	G	Y		V
I	O	T	A		E			G	L	E	E	
S		C		S	L	A	T				J	
E	C	H	O		A		T		E	W	E	R
	Z		U	N	D	R	E	S	S		C	
T	A	L	C		E		R		P	E	T	S
	R		H	O	N	E	S	T	Y		S	

58.

Words to find include ant, anti, author, **authoring**, auto, gnat, horn, hot, into, nag, nit, nth, oath, out, outing, rho, ring, roan, rot, roting, rout, routing, tag, tan, tang, tho, thorn, thou, tin, ting, tor and torn

56.

DEADLINE
NEATENED
EDITABLE
LEAPFROG
OGRESSES
ESCAPISM
SMARMIER

59.

- IMPROVISATION
- ARRANGEMENT
- ACCIDENTAL
- DISSONANCE
- INTERVAL

57.

- BAGEL
- NAAN
- CROISSANT
- BRIOCHE
- CIABATTA

60.

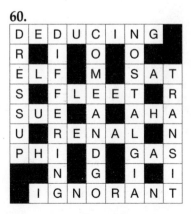

D	E	D	U	C	I	N	G	
R		I		O		O		
E	L	F		M		S	A	T
S		F	L	E	E	T		R
S	U	E		A		A	H	A
U		R	E	N	A	L		N
P	H	I		D		G	A	S
		N		G		I		I
	I	G	N	O	R	A	N	T

61.

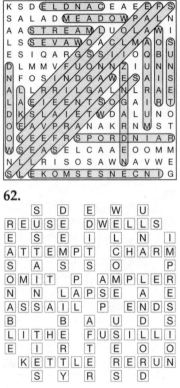

62.

```
        S   D   E   W   U
R E U S E   D W E L L S
E   S   E   I   L   N   I
A T T E M P T   C H A R M
S   A   S   S   O       P
O M I T   P   A M P L E R
N   N   L A P S E   A   E
A S S A I L   P   E N D S
B       B   A   U   D   S
L I T H E   F U S I L L I
E   I   R   T   E   O   O
  K E T T L E   R E R U N
    S   Y   R   S   D
```

63.
1. GAP
2. GASP
3. GAPES
4. GRAPES
5. GRASPED
6. UPGRADES

64.
- ESTUARY
- LAKE
- RAPIDS
- STREAM
- WATERFALL

65.
- 'The Kite Runner' by Khaled Hosseini
- 'The Girl with the Dragon Tattoo' by Stieg Larsson
- 'The Lovely Bones' by Alice Sebold
- 'The Handmaid's Tale' by Margaret Atwood
- 'The Bridges of Madison' County' by Robert James Waller

66.
- STOCK: LIVESTOCK and STOCKMARKET
- UP: UPTEMPO and TEMPORALLY
- HER: ARCHER and HERSELF
- SHOW: SIDESHOW and SHOWDOWN
- SEAS: OVERSEAS and SEASHELL

67.

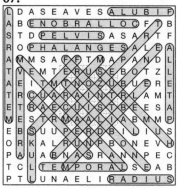

68.

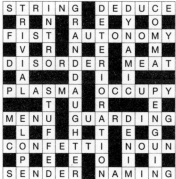

70.
The sixth fruit is APPLE:
- CHERRY + A
- BANANA + P
- PEACH + P
- ORANGE + L
- PLUM + E

71.

69.
Decode by replacing A with D, B with E, C with F and so on through to replacing Y with B and Z with C.
- GANYMEDE
- THEMISTO
- ADRASTEA
- THEBE
- IO

72.
- ENCOURAGE
- BELIEVE
- EMPOWER
- ATTAIN
- SUCCEED

73.

R	I	Ø	H	R	T	O	L	R	A
R	B	G	E	S	T	E	U	E	U
A	I	D	E	E	E	S	S	Z	I
N	W	P	E	R	S	I	A	N	L
O	S	R	O	I	I	C	N	T	D
K	Y	Y	A	P	O	Y	S	I	P
V	A	N	O	H	U	A	M	U	Y
L	U	R	E	C	Q	N	N	A	E
P	P	A	S	Y	R	E	R	I	H
R	E	S	C	T	U	K	N	N	P

74.

	S		A		L		E		B		C
	U	N	I	Q	U	E		V	O	U	C	H
	A		U		I	R	E		Z		A
J	I	G	S	A	W			R	A	Z	O	R
A		K				B		P		V	
B	E	L	I	E	F		A	R	E	N	A
S		E		O	W	L		E		I
	B	A	S	I	N		L	E	V	E	L	S
E		O		T				I		L
W	E	E	N	Y			H	U	M	A	N	E
I		V		O	A	T		D		V
S	U	I	N	G		U	T	O	P	I	A
H		L		A		X		N		D

75.

W	I	N	D	S	L	A	B
A	B	D	I	C	A	T	E
T	E	A	R	A	B	L	E
L	E	V	I	T	A	T	E
T	E	M	P	O	R	A	L
A	L	I	G	H	T	E	D
E	D	G	I	N	E	S	S

76.

Inward: 1-6 STOCKS; 7-13 EDITORS; 14-17 LOCO; 18-24 TORPEDO; 25-30 RECORD; 31-34 RATS; 35-39 UMBRA; 40-46 GRAMMAR; 47-50 GNAT. **Outward:** 50-44 TANGRAM; 43-41 MAR; 40-37 GARB; 36-30 MUSTARD; 29-27 ROC; 26-22 ERODE; 21-13 PROTOCOLS; 12-9 ROTI; 8-5 DESK; 4-1 COTS.

77.

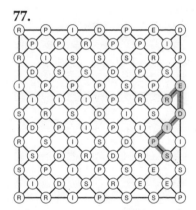

78.

79.

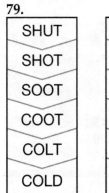

| SHUT |
| SHOT |
| SOOT |
| COOT |
| COLT |
| COLD |

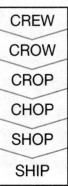

| CREW |
| CROW |
| CROP |
| CHOP |
| SHOP |
| SHIP |

80.
Words to find include cater, chair, charm, charr, cheer, claim, tater, tatie, their, there, therm, water, whare and where

82.

O	P	T	I	N	G		S	C	A	R	C	E
K		E		E		A		O		I		N
R	E	M	A	R	K	S		N	I	G	H	T
A		P		V		K		T		H		I
	G	E	N	E		E	L	E	C	T	O	R
W		S				W		N				E
A	L	T	E	R	S		U	T	M	O	S	T
N			E		S			D				Y
D	E	F	I	C	I	T		S	A	Y	S	
E		A		K		U		W		S		A
R	A	D	I	O		D	R	E	S	S	E	S
E		E		N		S		E		E		H
R	E	S	I	S	T		S	P	R	Y	L	Y

83.
1. RAG
2. CRAG
3. GRACE
4. CAGIER
5. GLACIER
6. ALLERGIC

81.

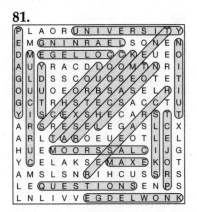

84.
- AUTHOR
- JUDGE
- PILOT
- TEACHER

SOLUTIONS

85.
Words to find include ace, acne, acre, act, antic, arc, article, cairn, can, cane, cant, canter, car, care, caret, cart, cartel, cat, cater, cent, central, certain, **certainly**, cite, city, clan, claret, clarinet, clarity, clay, clean, clear, cleat, client, crane, crate, cretin, cry, enact, ice, icy, lace, lacier, lacy, lance, lancer, lancet, larceny, latency, lice, literacy, lyric, nacre, nectar, nice, nicely, nicer, nicety, race, racily, racy, react, recant, recital, relic, rice, talc, trace, trance, trice

86.
- ART: IMPART and ARTWORK
- WIND: WHIRLWIND and WINDSWEPT
- NATION: STAGNATION and NATIONALLY
- CAPE: LANDSCAPE and CAPERED
- MUM: MINIMUM and MUMBLED

87.
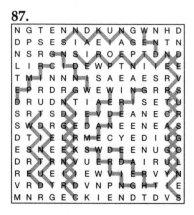

88.

89.
TEMPO

90.
- TREE
- DREAM
- CARBON
- BEGONIA
- PECUNIARY

91.

	F		S		S		C	
	L		E		A	T	O	P
B	A	H	T		R	A	D	
	M	E	T	R	I	C		F
	E	M	O			T	E	E
			G	U	I	L	T	
L	O	G		E		C	U	E
	P	L	O	T			D	
	T	O	N		A	R	I	A
	B	U	R	Y	I	N	G	
F	O	E	S		E	D	G	E

92.
- TEXT
- SOBS
- DEFEND
- SINUS
- ELSE

93.
1. PANTHER: times**pan ther**e
2. ALPACA: sc**alp, a ca**reless
3. POSSUM: tem**pos, sum**marizing
4. SALAMANDER: propo**sal, a man der**ailed
5. WEASEL: a**we as el**aborate

94.

95.

S	C	R	A	P		E	D	I	T	O	R	S
	O		F		E		I		O		E	
P	R	E	F	I	X	E	S		P	A	V	E
	G		A		H		C		A		I	
B	I	K	I	N	I		O	O	Z	E	S	
			R		L		N				E	
I	R	I	S		A	C	T		J	E	S	T
	E				R		I		O			
	Q	U	O	T	A		N	A	I	V	E	R
	U		N		T		U		N		N	
K	I	W	I		I	D	E	N	T	I	T	Y
	R		O		N		D		L		E	
T	E	E	N	A	G	E		M	Y	R	R	H

96.

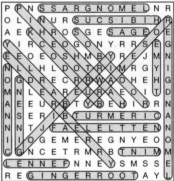

SOLUTIONS

97.
- BERET
- TRILBY
- FEDORA
- BASEBALL
- COWBOY

98.
Words to find include ail, aim, air, airs, airy, arm, iris, lair, lairs, lay, liar, liars, lira, mil, mils, mislay, rail, ray, rim, similar, **similarly**, sir, slay, slim and sly

99.
- CONGO RIVER BASIN
- AMAZONIA
- HAWAIIAN
- OLYMPIC
- BORNEO LOWLAND

100.

T	R	U	N	C	A	T	E	D
O		P		O		H		E
O	B	S	E	S	S	I	O	N
	A		L			N		S
C	H	A	M	P	A	G	N	E
O		C			S		U	
A	T	T	A	C	K	I	N	G
C		E		O		F		U
H	I	D	E	O	U	S	L	Y

101.

102.

103.
1. SAG
2. SNAG
3. GNATS
4. GRANTS
5. STRANGE
6. SERGEANT

104.
- CONCERT
- EXHIBITION
- FLIGHT
- LOTTERY
- MOVIE

105.
- 'Single Ladies (Put a Ring on It)' by Beyoncé
- 'Shake It Off' by Taylor Swift
- 'Rolling in the Deep' by Adele
- 'Poker Face' by Lady Gaga
- 'Call Me Maybe' by Carly Rae Jepsen

106.
- PROOF: FOOLPROOF and PROOFREAD
- DISH: BRANDISH and DISHWASHER
- HANDLE: MANHANDLE and HANDLEBAR
- WIND: WOODWIND and WINDMILL
- PENS: DAMPENS and PENSION

107.

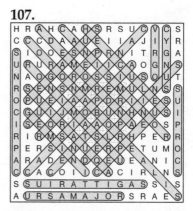

108.

109.
Decode by replacing A with L, B with M, C with N and so on through to replacing Y with J and Z with K:

- GRANDMOTHER
- DAUGHTER
- FATHER
- NEPHEW
- WIFE

110.
The sixth fish is PERCH:

- FLOUNDER + P
- COD + E
- CARP + R
- SNAPPER + C
- SALMON + H

111.

112.
- MONITOR LIZARD
- GIANT TORTOISE
- IGUANA
- SNAKE
- SKINK

113.

S	L	R	N	A	I	S	R	E	P
R	M	I	L	I	O	N	T	V	E
Y	T	L	G	R	C	A	N	C	E
S	O	O	I	H	N	P	I	A	L
Y	P	B	M	G	T	R	K	R	O
H	U	A	E	A	T	I	P	R	R
R	C	R	N	E	T	C	M	O	A
B	I	A	A	I	L	O	U	T	N
N	A	R	E	R	S	T	P	E	G
L	O	N	A	P	A	H	D	M	E

114.

115.

116.

Inward: 1-5 ELITE; 6-8 CUD;
9-12 EDGE; 13-19 PREDICT;
20-23 CURT; 24-28 SNIFF;
29-33 URGES; 34-38 IRATE;
39-42 ELSE; 43-45 TAT;
46-50 SAVED. **Outward**:
50-42 DEVASTATE; 41-37
SLEET; 36-32 ARISE; 31-27
GRUFF; 26-19 INSTRUCT;
18-14 CIDER; 13-11 PEG; 10-5
DEDUCE; 4-1 TILE.

117.

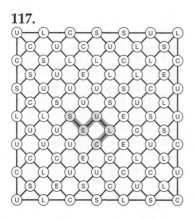

118.

119.

BOAR	PLOY
SOAR	PLOT
SOAK	CLOT
SOCK	COOT
SICK	COAT
KICK	COAX

120.

Words to find (including obscure words) include blain, blame, blare, blore, blume, blurs, boars, booms, boors, bourn, brain, brame, brome, bruin, brume, flame, flams, flare, flume, foams, fours, frame, frore, frorn, glams, glare, gloms, glume, glums, grain, grame, grams, groin and grume

121.

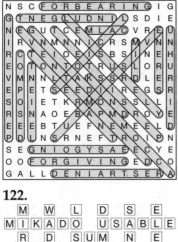

122.

```
 M   W   L   D   S       E
M I K A D O   U S A B L E
 R   D   S U M   N   E
A R R I V E   M   G I V E
 O       S P Y       E
D R O V E   I   P L A N S
 A   B E A T S   R
S H R U B   N   I T C H Y
 O       G O D       A
E P I C   R   E A S I N G
 P   A   O R B   T   D
B E S T O W   U N I T E D
 R   S   N   G   R   D
```

123.
1. TAG
2. GAIT
3. GIANT
4. EATING
5. TEAMING
6. MAGNETIC

124.
- ARCHERY
- GOLF
- SKIING
- TENNIS

125.
Words to find include abode, ado, adobe, adore, adored, boa, boar, board, boarded, bob, bode, boded, bomb, bombard, **bombarded**, bombed, bomber, bore, bored, broad, dado, doe, doer, dome, domed, mob, mobbed, mode, more, oar, oared, odd, odder, ode, orb, ore, redo, road, roadbed, roam, roamed, rob, robbed, robe, robed, rod, rode and roe

126.
- SIGHT: OVERSIGHT and SIGHTLESS
- MUFF: EARMUFF and MUFFIN
- BASE: DATABASE and BASELINE
- NUMERIC: ALPHANUMERIC and NUMERICALLY
- BED: BOBBED and BEDBUG

127.

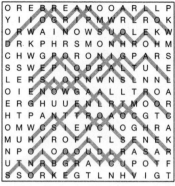

128.

129.
QUICK

130.
- NUDGE
- COSMOS
- DILEMMA
- VIBRATION
- PARALLEL

131.

	B		S		D		P	
	A		C		A	P	S	E
U	N	D	E	R	W	A	Y	
	Y	E	N		N	I	C	E
	A	T	E			R	H	O
O	N	E		Y		S	I	N
		R	E	A	R		A	
		M	A	W		S	T	Y
S	W	I	G		G	U	R	U
		N	E	W		M	I	C
P	E	E	R		H	O	C	K

132.
- EYRIE
- SITS
- TRYST
- ROWER
- LAPEL

133.
1. RICKSHAW: t**ricks haw**ks
2. TRAILER: con**trail er**upted
3. SLEDGE: mi**sled, ge**nerally
4. TANDEM: ran**t, and em**otions
5. COACH: dis**co, ach**ing

134.

135.

136.

F	R	U	I	T	F	U	L

U	L	T	E	R	I	O	R

O	R	D	A	I	N	E	D

E	D	I	F	I	C	E	S

E	S	C	H	E	W	A	L

A	L	I	E	N	A	T	E

T	E	M	E	R	I	T	Y

137.
- BOWL
- FUNNEL
- SAUCEPAN
- GRATER
- MASHER

138.
Words to find include emit, emits, ins, inset, ion, ions, its, men, met, mine, mines, mint, mints, mist, moist, money, nest, net, nit, nits, noise, noisy, omen, omens, omit, omits, one, ones, onset, semi, sent, set, sin, sine, sit, stint, ten, tens, tent, tents, test, **testimony**, time, times, tin, tine, tines, tins, tint, tiny, yen, yens, yes and yet

139.
- GIRAFFE
- MONGOOSE
- GAZELLE
- BABOON
- LEMUR

142.

O	B	S	E	S	S		S	P	E	E	C	H
A		X		P		A		L		H		
P	L	E	A		I	N	C	L	U	D	E	D
S		M		R				D		A		
P	A	N	I	N	I		S	L	E	E	P	S
N		T		Y				L				
I	D	L	E		U	R	N		K	E	Y	S
E			A		D		I					
P	L	U	R	A	L		I	N	D	E	N	T
A		E		C		D		O				
H	Y	S	T	E	R	I	A		I	N	N	S
E		R		A		T		N		E		
I	D	I	O	C	Y		E	I	G	H	T	H

140.

S	N	O	B		G		
E			A	P	E	S	S
A	R	M	Y		M	E	L	T
			O		M		A
D	E	B	U	G	G	I	N	G
O		A		R			
C	O	W	S		O	W	E	S
K		L	I	R	A		U
			M		N	E	O	N

141.

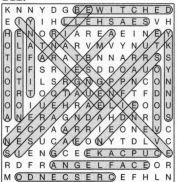

143.
1. VIA
2. VAIN
3. NAIVE
4. NAVIES
5. NATIVES
6. VINTAGES

144.
- GLOVES
- SHEARS
- SPADE
- TROWEL
- WHEELBARROW

145.
- Animal Crossing: New Horizons
- The Legend of Zelda: Breath of the Wild
- Castlevania: Symphony of the Night
- Halo: Combat Evolved
- Star Wars: Knights of the Old Republic

146.
- DIVE: SKYDIVE and DIVESTING
- FRUIT: GRAPEFRUIT and FRUITLESS
- TEE: COMMITTEE and TEETOTAL
- OWNER: HOMEOWNER and OWNERSHIP
- SHOE: HORSESHOE and SHOESTRING

147.

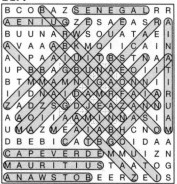

148.

149.
Decode by replacing A with S, B with T, C with U and so on through to replacing Y with Q and Z with R:
- MEDITATION
- EXERCISE
- BALANCE
- FOCUS
- POSE

150.
The sixth clothing item is a CLOAK:
- BLOUSE + C
- JACKET + L
- SOCKS + O
- SUIT + A
- DRESS + K